D1171935

THE ENCYCLOPEDIA OF PSYCHOACTIVE DRUGS

SERIES 1

SERIES 2

THE ORIGINS & SOURCES OF DRUGS

OF DRUGS

GENERAL EDITOR
Professor Solomon H. Snyder, M.D.

*Distinguished Service Professor of
Neuroscience, Pharmacology, and Psychiatry at
The Johns Hopkins University School of Medicine*

•

ASSOCIATE EDITOR
Professor Barry L. Jacobs, Ph.D.

*Program in Neuroscience, Department of Psychology,
Princeton University*

•

SENIOR EDITORIAL CONSULTANT
Joann Rodgers

*Deputy Director, Office of Public Affairs at
The Johns Hopkins Medical Institutions*

THE ENCYCLOPEDIA OF PSYCHOACTIVE DRUGS

SERIES 2

THE ORIGINS & SOURCES OF DRUGS

ALAN THEODORE

CHELSEA HOUSE PUBLISHERS

NEW YORK • PHILADELPHIA

EDITOR-IN-CHIEF: Nancy Toff
EXECUTIVE EDITOR: Remmel T. Nunn
MANAGING EDITOR: Karyn Gullen Browne
COPY CHIEF: Juliann Barbato
PICTURE EDITOR: Adrian G. Allen
ART DIRECTOR: Giannella Garrett
MANUFACTURING MANAGER: Gerald Levine

Staff for THE ORIGINS AND SOURCES OF DRUGS:

SENIOR EDITOR: Jane Larkin Crain
ASSOCIATE EDITOR: Paula Edelson
ASSISTANT EDITOR: Laura-Ann Dolce
COPY EDITORS: Karen Hammonds, James Guiry
DEPUTY COPY CHIEF: Ellen Scordato
EDITORIAL ASSISTANT: Susan DeRosa
ASSOCIATE PICTURE EDITOR: Juliette Dickstein
PICTURE RESEARCHER: Susan Quist
DESIGNER: Victoria Tomaselli
DESIGN ASSISTANT: Laura Lang
PRODUCTION COORDINATOR: Joseph Romano
COVER ILLUSTRATION: Art Resource

Library of Congress Cataloging in Publication Data

Theodore, Alan.
   The Origins and Sources of Drugs.

   (The Encyclopedia of psychoactive drugs. Series 2)
   Bibliography: p.
   Includes index.
   Summary: Describes the characteristics and effects of various drugs derived
from plants.
   1. Psychotropic drugs—Juvenile literature.
2. Psychotropic plants—Juvenile literature.
[1. Psychotropic drugs. 2. Psychotropic
plants. 3. Drugs] I. Title. II. Series.
RM315.T427 1988   615'.78   87-35233

ISBN 1-55546-234-0

0-7910-0806-1 (pbk.)

CONTENTS

Tobacco heir Patrick Reynolds, grandson of the founder of the R. J. Reynolds Tobacco Company, gives cigarettes the thumbs down. Reynolds says he went public with his attack on smoking to try to save lives.

FOREWORD

In the Mainstream
of American Life

One of the legacies of the social upheaval of the 1960s is that psychoactive drugs have become part of the mainstream of American life. Schools, homes, and communities cannot be "drug proofed." There is a demand for drugs — and the supply is plentiful. Social norms have changed and drugs are not only available—they are everywhere.

But where efforts to curtail the supply of drugs and outlaw their use have had tragically limited effects on demand, it may be that education has begun to stem the rising tide of drug abuse among young people and adults alike.

Over the past 25 years, as drugs have become an increasingly routine facet of contemporary life, a great many teenagers have adopted the notion that drug taking was somehow a right or a privilege or a necessity. They have done so, however, without understanding the consequences of drug use during the crucial years of adolescence.

The teenage years are few in the total life cycle, but critical in the maturation process. During these years adolescents face the difficult tasks of discovering their identity, clarifying their sexual roles, asserting their independence, learning to cope with authority, and searching for goals that will give their lives meaning.

Drugs rob adolescents of precious time, stamina, and health. They interrupt critical learning processes, sometimes forever. Teenagers who use drugs are likely to withdraw increasingly into themselves, to "cop out" at just the time when they most need to reach out and experience the world.

Schoolyards have become a breeding ground for drug and alcohol abuse, as more and more illicit substances have become readily available.

Fortunately, as a recent Gallup poll shows, young people are beginning to realize this, too. They themselves label drugs their most important problem. In the last few years, moreover, the climate of tolerance and ignorance surrounding drugs has been changing.

Adolescents as well as adults are becoming aware of mounting evidence that every race, ethnic group, and class is vulnerable to drug dependency.

Recent publicity about the cost and failure of drug rehabilitation efforts; dangerous drug use among pilots, air traffic controllers, star athletes, and Hollywood celebrities; and drug-related accidents, suicides, and violent crime have focused the public's attention on the need to wage an all-out war on drug abuse before it seriously undermines the fabric of society itself.

The anti-drug message is getting stronger and there is evidence that the message is beginning to get through to adults and teenagers alike.

The Encyclopedia of Psychoactive Drugs hopes to play a part in the national campaign now under way to educate young people about drugs. Series 1 provides clear and comprehensive discussions of common psychoactive substances, outlines their psychological and physiological effects on the mind and body, explains how they "hook" the user, and separates fact from myth in the complex issue of drug abuse.

Whereas Series 1 focuses on specific drugs, such as nicotine or cocaine, Series 2 confronts a broad range of both social and physiological phenomena. Each volume addresses the ramifications of drug use and abuse on some aspect of human experience: social, familial, cultural, historical, and physical. Separate volumes explore questions about the effects of drugs on brain chemistry and unborn children; the use and abuse of painkillers; the relationship between drugs and sexual behavior, sports, and the arts; drugs and disease; the role of drugs in history; and the sophisticated drugs now being developed in the laboratory that will profoundly change the future.

Each book in the series is fully illustrated and is tailored to the needs and interests of young readers. The more adolescents know about drugs and their role in society, the less likely they are to misuse them.

Joann Rodgers
Senior Editorial Consultant

An Assyrian carving of a man holding a poppy plant. Opium and morphine, derived from the poppy, have been used for thousands of years both to control pain and to induce altered states of consciousness.

INTRODUCTION

The Gift of Wizardry
Use and Abuse

JACK H. MENDELSON, M.D.
NANCY K. MELLO, Ph.D.
Alcohol and Drug Abuse Research Center
Harvard Medical School—McLean Hospital

Dorothy to the Wizard:

"I think you are a very bad man," said Dorothy.
"Oh no, my dear; I'm really a very good man; but I'm a very bad Wizard."
—from THE WIZARD OF OZ

Man is endowed with the gift of wizardry, a talent for discovery and invention. The discovery and invention of substances that change the way we feel and behave are among man's special accomplishments, and, like so many other products of our wizardry, these substances have the capacity to harm as well as to help. Psychoactive drugs can cause profound changes in the chemistry of the brain and other vital organs, and although their legitimate use can relieve pain and cure disease, their abuse leads in a tragic number of cases to destruction.

Consider alcohol — available to all and yet regarded with intense ambivalence from biblical times to the present day. The use of alcoholic beverages dates back to our earliest ancestors. Alcohol use and misuse became associated with the worship of gods and demons. One of the most powerful Greek gods was Dionysus, lord of fruitfulness and god of wine. The Romans adopted Dionysus but changed his name to Bacchus. Festivals and holidays associated with Bacchus celebrated the harvest and the origins of life. Time has blurred the images of the Bacchanalian festival, but the theme of drunkenness as a major part of celebration has survived the pagan gods and remains a familiar part of modern society. The term "Bacchanalian Festival" conveys a more appealing image than "drunken orgy" or "pot party," but whatever the label, drinking alcohol is a form of drug use that results in addiction for millions.

The fact that many millions of other people can use alcohol in moderation does not mitigate the toll this drug takes on society as a whole. According to reliable estimates, one out of every ten Americans develops a serious alcohol-related problem sometime in his or her lifetime. In addition, automobile accidents caused by drunken drivers claim the lives of tens of thousands every year. Many of the victims are gifted young people, just starting out in adult life. Hospital emergency rooms abound with patients seeking help for alcohol-related injuries.

Who is to blame? Can we blame the many manufacturers who produce such an amazing variety of alcoholic beverages? Should we blame the educators who fail to explain the perils of intoxication, or so exaggerate the dangers of drinking that no one could possibly believe them? Are friends to blame — those peers who urge others to "drink more and faster," or the macho types who stress the importance of being able to "hold your liquor"? Casting blame, however, is hardly constructive, and pointing the finger is a fruitless way to deal with the problem. Alcoholism and drug abuse have few culprits but many victims. Accountability begins with each of us, every time we choose to use or misuse an intoxicating substance.

It is ironic that some of man's earliest medicines, derived from natural plant products, are used today to poison and to intoxicate. Relief from pain and suffering is one of society's many continuing goals. Over 3,000 years ago, the Therapeutic Papyrus of Thebes, one of our earliest written records, gave instructions for the use of opium in the treatment of pain. Opium, in the form of its major derivative, morphine, and similar compounds, such as heroin, have also been used by many to induce changes in mood and feeling. Another example of man's misuse of a natural substance is the coca leaf, which for centuries was used by the Indians of Peru to reduce fatigue and hunger. Its modern derivative, cocaine, has important medical use as a local anesthetic. Unfortunately, its increasing abuse in the 1980s clearly has reached epidemic proportions.

The purpose of this series is to explore in depth the psychological and behavioral effects that psychoactive drugs have on the individual, and also, to investigate the ways in which drug use influences the legal, economic, cultural, and even moral aspects of societies. The information presented here (and in other books in this series) is based on many clinical and laboratory studies and other observations by people from diverse walks of life.

Over the centuries, novelists, poets, and dramatists have provided us with many insights into the sometimes seductive but ultimately problematic aspects of alcohol and drug use. Physicians, lawyers, biologists, psychologists, and social scientists have contributed to a better understanding of the causes and consequences of using these substances. The authors in this series have attempted to gather and condense all the latest information about drug use and abuse. They have also described the sometimes wide gaps in our knowledge and have suggested some new ways to answer many difficult questions.

One such question, for example, is how do alcohol and drug problems get started? And what is the best way to treat them when they do? Not too many years ago, alcoholics and drug abusers were regarded as evil, immoral, or both. It is now recognized that these persons suffer from very complicated diseases involving deep psychological and social problems. To understand how the disease begins and progresses, it is necessary to understand the nature of the substance, the behavior of addicts, and the characteristics of the society or culture in which they live.

Although many of the social environments we live in are very similar, some of the most subtle differences can strongly influence our thinking and behavior. Where we live, go to school and work, whom we discuss things with — all influence our opinions about drug use and misuse. Yet we also share certain commonly accepted beliefs that outweigh any differences in our attitudes. The authors in this series have tried to identify and discuss the central, most crucial issues concerning drug use and misuse.

Despite the increasing sophistication of the chemical substances we create in the laboratory, we have a long way to go in our efforts to make these powerful drugs work for us rather than against us.

The volumes in this series address a wide range of timely questions. What influence has drug use had on the arts? Why do so many of today's celebrities and star athletes use drugs, and what is being done to solve this problem? What is the relationship between drugs and crime? What is the physiological basis for the power drugs can hold over us? These are but a few of the issues explored in this far-ranging series.

Educating people about the dangers of drugs can go a long way toward minimizing the desperate consequences of substance abuse for individuals and society as a whole. Luckily, human beings have the resources to solve even the most serious problems that beset them, once they make the commitment to do so. As one keen and sensitive observer, Dr. Lewis Thomas, has said,

> There is nothing at all absurd about the human condition. We matter. It seems to me a good guess, hazarded by a good many people who have thought about it, that we may be engaged in the formation of something like a mind for the life of this planet. If this is so, we are still at the most primitive stage, still fumbling with language and thinking, but infinitely capacitated for the future. Looked at this way, it is remarkable that we've come as far as we have in so short a period, really no time at all as geologists measure time. We are the newest, youngest, and the brightest thing around.

THE
ORIGINS & SOURCES
OF DRUGS

A 16th-century French engraving shows pharmacists at work in a medicinal-herb garden. Most of the naturally derived psychoactive drugs were first valued for their therapeutic properties.

AUTHOR'S PREFACE

The dawn of civilization may have occurred when primitive people realized that they could have a steady and reliable food source by growing things in the earth. Soon after this discovery, they found that plant life yielded more than just nutritional sustenance. By ingesting the nuts, fruits, or leaves of certain plants they could see strange and wonderful things and experience strange and wonderful sensations.

Ancient civilizations put this knowledge to different uses. Some cultures believed that eating organic hallucinogenic drugs could bring them new spiritual awareness and used these substances for religious and ceremonial purposes. The ancient Aztecs, for example, an Indian tribe in Mexico before the Spanish settled there, used the psychoactive component of the peyote cactus as an integral part of their religious ritual. The ancient Greeks used another psychoactive drug, alcohol, for similar purposes. Several times a year the Greeks celebrated the rites of Dionysus, the god of the vine, with festivals fueled by tremendous amounts of wine.

Naturally derived psychoactive drugs were also valued for their medicinal uses. Opium, the psychoactive juice of the poppy plant, has been used as an analgesic, or painkiller,

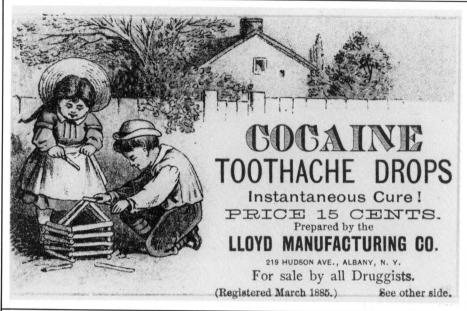

A 19th-century advertisement for a preparation containing cocaine. During this era patent medicines were routinely laced with cocaine and opiates; they could be purchased over the counter and through the mail.

since ancient times, and morphine, its derivative, is one of the most powerful drugs for the relief of pain. Cocaine, which is best known in the 1980s as a highly dangerous recreational drug, was touted in the 19th century as a virtual panacea for a wide variety of ailments.

Unfortunately, virtually all of these organic, or plant-derived, psychoactive drugs are subject to abuse. When this happens, the very substances that had been used effectively by some for spiritual and physical well-being can endanger the health, and sometimes the life, of the abuser. Some of these drugs, such as heroin and cocaine, are illicit substances that are well known to be highly addictive. Other substances, however, are legal drugs that are not as notorious for being dangerous. Drinking alcohol, for example, is an extremely popular—and legal (for those over 21)—pastime in the United States. What many people do not know, however, is that alcohol is responsible for more than 30,000 deaths in the United States each year. Perhaps even more surprising is the recent evidence that caffeine, the active ingredient in coffee—America's most popular beverage—is an addictive substance with some abuse potential.

This book explores the histories, sources, origins, and natures of both legal and illicit organic drugs. Each chapter examines the effects—both good and bad—and the history of a specific psychoactive substance. Also included is a discussion of where the drug grows and where it is processed, or separated, from the plant. Readers will also learn what sort of restrictions are placed on the use of legal drugs and of the efforts being made to halt the manufacture, sale, and use of illegal ones.

Vin Mariani, a wine that contained a liberal dose of cocaine, was touted during the 19th century as a mood elevator. The wine was praised for its curative properties by such notables as Thomas Edison and Pope Leo XIII.

CHAPTER 1

COCAINE

Abuse of the stimulant drug cocaine has become a problem of epidemic proportions during the 1980s. Although the drug is illegal, it is fairly easy — albeit expensive — to obtain; this fact, coupled with cocaine's glamorous image as the drug of choice for the rich and famous, has given this substance a great deal of allure. In the 1980s, a more concentrated, highly addictive form of cocaine known as crack has become a popular street drug, and the circle of its abusers has since expanded to include all classes and age groups.

The immediate effect of cocaine is an intense euphoria, a decrease in hunger, an indifference to pain, and an illusion of great physical strength and mental capacity. Most users take cocaine primarily for its mood-elevating property. This exhilarating effect does not last long, however, and is almost invariably followed by depression. The user will then crave more cocaine to restore the euphoria. This cycle can become a repeated pattern, and if it does it means that the user has become psychologically dependent on the drug.

Cocaine is derived from the coca plant, *Erythroxylon coca*. The history of the use of this plant dates back to the beginnings of the Inca empire in what is now Peru during the 12th century, C.E. (although some sources say that Indians

A ceramic vessel depicting a deity of a Peruvian Indian tribe holding a lime bottle and a coca bag. Many Peruvian Indians considered coca a gift from the gods and chewed its leaves during religious rituals.

were using coca before the rise of the Incas, perhaps as early as 3000 B.C.E.). (C.E. and B.C.E. correspond to A.D. and B.C., respectively.) The Incas considered the coca plant a gift from the gods and chewed its leaves during religious rituals, burials, and for other spiritual purposes.

Modern use of cocaine began in the mid-19th century, when the psychoactive ingredient was isolated from the organic plant. During this time scientists and doctors, including the Viennese physician and pioneer psychoanalyst Sigmund Freud, touted cocaine as a medicinal cure-all that could treat anything from gastrointestinal disorders to morphine addiction and depression. Cocaine was sold by apothecary shops and through the mail without a doctor's prescription as a tonic, an antidepressant, and a local anesthetic. Sadly, cocaine proved to be anything but a medical miracle. Evidence of its dangerous properties is still accumulating, and its sole medical use is as a topical anesthetic.

Cultivation, Processing, and Refining

The coca bush is a deciduous shrub (a plant that sheds its leaves at the end of the growing season) that is grown on the eastern slopes of the Andes Mountains in Bolivia and Peru, and in the Amazon Basin of Brazil. To speed up the growing period, most farmers purchase 18-month-old seedlings rather than start from scratch with seeds. Intensive cultivation is the usual practice, with 40,000 coca seedlings planted per *hectare* (2.47 acres) of land. If properly cared for, with weed and insect control and adequate fertilization, the coca bush can yield as many as six harvests of leaves a year.

Following these harvests, the leaves are dried, either in the sun or in large commercial driers. The leaves are then converted to coca paste, either by the farmers or by middlemen who purchase the leaves. These workers place the leaves in pits dug in the ground and treat them with kerosene,

Peasants cultivate coca shrubs in the Andes Mountains in Bolivia. Farmers often plant as many as 40,000 coca seedlings per hectare, and with proper care each bush can yield as many as 6 harvests a year.

Workers in Colombia transform coca leaves into paste. Laboratory processing will then derive cocaine base and cocaine itself from this paste.

sulfuric acid, and calcium carbonate. The chemical reaction that ensues extracts a paste from the leaf. The paste, which contains the *alkaloid* (active principal) of the plant, is the raw material of cocaine.

The paste is then wrapped in burlap bags and sold to intermediaries, who in turn sell it to the processor for refining. The refining process, which takes place in laboratories hidden away in the Amazon and other remote areas of Colombia and Bolivia, produces a "washed" and purer form of the paste that is the cocaine base.

From the laboratories, cocaine is shipped by boat or plane to small cays or inlets in the Caribbean where refueling, repair, and transshipment facilities are located. Here it is transferred to small boats or private planes for smuggling into the United States. Private individuals, including couriers for the drug syndicates, also smuggle cocaine into the United States on commercial airline flights.

The High Profits of Smuggling

The drug derived from the coca bush has turned the plant into a major but illegal cash crop and an important factor in the economy of several Latin American countries. In Bolivia, for example, the illicit export of cocaine has become a business three times more important than the nation's leading legitimate export, tin. The cocaine traffic pumps more than $500 million into the economy of this economically depressed nation. In Colombia, the smuggling of cocaine and other drugs brings more income into the country than does coffee. And the annual cocaine output in Peru is worth a staggering $650 million.

Smuggling cocaine into the United States from Latin America can be a process as elaborate as producing the drug itself and is becoming more difficult as law enforcement officials work on more sophisticated systems to detect these crimes. Many sneak the drug through customs by "body-

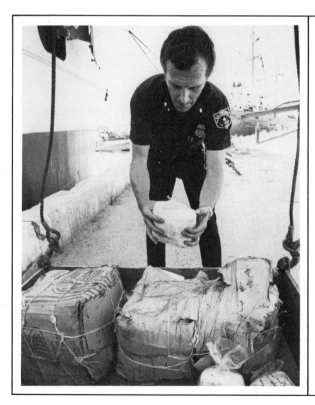

A U.S. Customs control officer examines a bag of cocaine confiscated in Miami, Florida. Miami is considered the major point of entry for most of the cocaine entering the United States.

packing," or storing, the cocaine in their stomachs or intestinal tracts in condoms, balloons, or other receptacles. The containers occasionally break or leak their contents, which can cause an overdose. These accidents are a major source of cocaine deaths in this country.

Other smugglers depend on accomplices. In September 1986, several baggage handlers at Miami International Airport and airline officials at Kennedy International Airport in New York were indicted for aiding and abetting cocaine smugglers.

A major portion of the cocaine distributed in the United States enters the country through Miami, Florida. Indeed, approximately 25 percent of all the cocaine seizures in the country occur at Miami International Airport.

Further indication that Miami is a center for the profitable cocaine trade comes from statistics compiled by the Federal Reserve System, the federal banking organization that has wide powers to control credit and the flow of money. The Miami branch of the Federal Reserve Bank of Atlanta was the only branch of the system to show a cash surplus — $4.75 billion—in 1980.

The War on Cocaine Production

With the support of the United States, the cocaine-producing countries of Latin America are taking actions to stop the cocaine trade. In Peru, for example, the government tries to limit the cultivation of the coca bush to meet domestic consumption needs for the leaf, as well as for legitimate medicinal uses of cocaine. (In Peru and other South American countries, workers chew the coca leaf as a palliative against hunger and exhaustion.)

Bolivia is another country that has cooperated with the United States in an effort to halt cocaine production. In 1986, Bolivia began a campaign to search out and destroy the estimated three dozen laboratories that process much of the 32,000 tons of coca leaves harvested there each year.

The United States participated in this project, which was known as "Operation Blast Furnace," by supplying 6 army helicopters, several transport planes, trucks, and about 160 men. In the initial raid, a laboratory capable of producing 2,200 pounds of cocaine a week was located, seized, and destroyed.

Thus far, these attempts to stop the cocaine trade have been hardly more than symbolic. The drug trade in Colombia, Bolivia, and other cocaine-producing countries is controlled by powerful gangster syndicates. The leaders are billionaires, able to corrupt government officials and influence public opinion in their favor. Sometimes, they even manage to purchase respectability. In Medellin, Colombia, a center of cocaine activity in Latin America, the head of a powerful cocaine syndicate built a zoo for the city and a housing project for the poor.

When the drug traffickers encounter resistance, however, they resort to violence and terrorism. For example, on November 7, 1985, a guerrilla force in league with the drug syndicates seized the Palace of Justice in Bogota, Colombia, destroying all documents relating to pending extraditions of drug traffickers and killing all 24 justices of the Supreme Court of Colombia. In the same month, 19 members of a U.S.-supported program to destroy coca plants in the Peruvian jungles were ambushed and killed by drug traffickers.

In addition to the drug traffickers themselves, the peasants who grow the coca bush form a strong center of resistance to suppression of cocaine production. In theory, these peasants must sell their coca leaves to a government agency, *Empresa Nacional de la Coca* (ENACO), and the amount of acreage that can be devoted to coca bush cultivation is restricted. However, many peasants do not register with ENACO but sell their leaves instead to drug traffickers who pay much more. In attempting to control this trend, in 1987 the U.S. Drug Enforcement Administration (DEA) began administering a 5-year, $56 million crop substitution program to peasants who give up coca plant cultivation. This has not provided much incentive for peasants, who can earn much more growing coca than the $140 a year they would receive for substituting another crop.

Despite these obstacles, the DEA, working with Latin American governments, hopes to eventually stop the cocaine trade. Recognizing that past campaigns to eradicate the coca plant crops have not been effective, the strategy now is to concentrate on the drug middlemen. By putting coca purchasers, processors, and dealers out of business, the officials hope to make the crop unprofitable and thus force the peasants to switch to other crops.

A U.S. aircraft surveys the U.S.-Mexico border. Surveillance gaps in that 1,900-mile border make it a tempting route of entry for drug traffickers.

The U.S. government has used foreign aid as a means of prodding Latin American governments into cooperating with the anticocaine program. In August 1986, Congress passed a foreign aid bill stating that the United States will send financial assistance to a cocaine-producing nation only if that country has shown some degree of success in combating this problem.

The U.S. government is also combating the drug syndicate chieftains based in Colombia. In 1979, these two countries signed a treaty stating that American cocaine traffickers living in Colombia could be deported to the United States, and vice versa.

Protecting U.S. Borders

To date, the attempt to prevent airborne smugglers from sneaking cocaine and other drugs into the United States has not been successful. According to one estimate, only 10% of flights smuggling cocaine are intercepted.

In addition, the points of entry for smugglers have spread from south Florida to the length of the 1,900-mile U.S. border with Mexico. Huge gaps in radar surveillance of the border make this a tempting route of entry for traffickers. "There are spots where you could fly across in an aircraft the size of the U.S. Capitol and never be detected," is how one U.S. congressman described the situation.

Contributing to inadequate control of the border is the lack of coordination among the DEA, the Customs Service, and other concerned agencies. Although the Customs Service has a small force of patrol planes, this fleet is not large enough to do the job. The U.S. government is preparing a new national drug interdiction policy in an attempt to remedy the situation. If the funds are appropriated by Congress, seven "aerostats" (huge radar-equipped balloons), augmented by Air Force C-130 transport planes and helicopters, will soon patrol what is now an easily penetrated Mexican-American border. Perhaps this will be the first step in controlling — and someday ending—the profitable and perilous cocaine trade.

A drawing of the Cannabis sativa *plant, from which marijuana is derived.
The drug itself is actually a combination of the leaves, stems, and
flowering tops of the plant, all of which are psychoactive.*

CHAPTER 2

PRODUCTS OF THE INDIAN HEMP PLANT

The Indian hemp plant marijuana, the world's most commonly used hallucinogen, comes from a weedlike plant called *Cannabis sativa*. "Marijuana" actually refers to the psychoactive leaves, stems, and flowering tops of the plant.

The psychoactive component in *Cannabis sativa* is a chemical called tetrahydrocannabinol, or THC, that acts upon a receptor in the brain that controls consciousness. The highest concentration of THC is found in the resin of the plant.

Doses of marijuana with even a low THC content (approximately 2%) affect mood, mental perceptions, fine and gross motor coordination, blood pressure, and pulse rate. Users typically experience a relaxed euphoric feeling and a desire to sleep. Even at this relatively low dose, the drug distorts sensory perception and impairs coordination; driving or using dangerous machinery under the influence of marijuana is not recommended. Higher doses of marijuana may produce hallucinations, delusions, and feelings of persecution.

History of Marijuana

The first recorded description of marijuana appeared in a Chinese medical book in the second century, B.C.E. The Chinese had used the hemp plant as raw material for rope 2,000 years earlier. The ancient Persians, Greeks, Romans, East Indians, and Assyrians were other groups in which the therapeutic value of marijuana was recognized; many of these peoples used the drug to control muscle spasms, to reduce pain, and to treat indigestion.

There is evidence that marijuana was used for its psychoactive properties in Asia as early as 1500 B.C.E. According to ancient Indian folklore, the Hindu god Siva brought the marijuana plant down from the Himalayan mountains for the pleasure of the Aryans, who had invaded India. Other cultures used the cannabis plant for recreational purposes as well. In 1155 B.C.E., according to Arab legend, a religious leader named Haydar discovered the plant, ate some of its leaves, and became euphoric. Although Europeans heard tales of the intoxicating properties of the hemp plant from world travelers such as Marco Polo, cannabis was not a commonly used drug in Europe until Napoleon's army occupied Egypt and discovered hashish there in the 18th century. When they sent samples of the drug (described in detail later in this chapter) back to France, it sparked new awareness of hallucinatory drugs in Europe.

A sculpture of the Hindu god Siva. According to ancient Indian folklore, Siva brought the marijuana plant down from the Himalayan mountains for the pleasure of the Aryans, who had invaded India.

A Sicilian rope maker tests the quality of his products. The hemp plant was originally cultivated for use in the manufacture of rope and twine.

Marijuana in the United States

The hemp plant was originally cultivated in the American colonies during the early 17th century as raw material for making rope, twine, and coarse woven cloth. Soon thereafter, the medicinal properties of the plant were discovered, and in the 19th century the drug was used for the treatment of ailments ranging from headaches and insomnia to labor pains and menstrual cramps.

Around this time the recreational use of marijuana was introduced into the United States by Mexican workers who crossed the border into Texas. The habit soon spread to other southwestern states and was quite popular among the jazz musicians who congregated in New Orleans in the period after World War I. As jazz spread throughout the country, so did the use of marijuana among its adherents — both musicians and audiences.

At this time, there was little precise scientific knowledge concerning marijuana. There were all kinds of opinions with no facts to back them up. To some, marijuana was the "killer weed — a powerful narcotic in which lurks murder, insanity and death," to quote from a poster of the era. Others thought it was a harmless substance. And some thought it had positive effects, such as increasing sexual potency. However, usage was confined to an extremely small segment of the population.

The popularity of marijuana soared in the lenient and experimental 1960s, becoming widespread on college campuses and among young adults. The trend continued in the 1970s; by 1979, it was estimated that 68% of young adults aged 18 to 25 had tried marijuana at least once, and 31% of adolescents aged 13 to 17 had used it once or more. Use of marijuana has declined in the 1980s, however, as evidence regarding the dangers of the drug has accumulated.

Botanical Properties

Cannabis sativa is a hardy plant can grow almost anywhere, but the plants that contain the most THC, and are therefore the most potent, grow best in climates that are hot and dry. Thus, marijuana grown in Mexico and other Latin American countries has more powerful effects than does the cannabis plant grown in the United States.

Modern horticultural science has made possible the cultivation of cannabis that is 10 to 30 times more potent than the older varieties. By using selective genetics and new propagation techniques, higher grades of cannabis have been produced that bear little resemblance to the relatively mild marijuana in common use during the 1960s and 1970s.

One of these varieties is Sinsemilla, meaning "without seeds" in Spanish. It is so named because this variety is cultivated by weeding out the female plants before they are pollinated. If the female plant is not pollinated, it produces a greater amount of the sticky resin, which in turn contains a higher concentration of THC. Sinsemilla can contain as much as 5% more THC than normally pollinated marijuana.

The Second Largest Cash Crop

Although Colombia, Jamaica, Mexico, and other Latin American and Caribbean countries are the major suppliers of marijuana to the United States, cannabis cultivation in this country has also become an important if illegal agricultural

Marijuana became a popular drug during the late 1960s, when many young Americans began smoking it in part as a gesture of protest against establishment values.

pursuit. In fact, marijuana is, after corn, the second largest cash crop in the United States. In 1984, domestically produced marijuana was worth $16.6 billion, with each plant worth $2,000 to $3,000 on the market.

Because growing marijuana has become so profitable, it has expanded from a small, usually private, enterprise to a big business controlled by organized crime. In order to avoid detection, planters grow the cannabis along stream beds, in areas screened by trees, in narrow rows difficult to spot from the air, in isolated backwoods areas, and even in national forests.

These criminal enterprises are also prepared to protect their illegal crops with weapons. Some mine their cannabis patches with booby traps. The presence of armed criminals — who are determined to protect what they consider their territorial rights — in woods and forests has endangered the lives of hikers and campers who inadvertently wander into these areas.

There have been a number of reports of such incidents. Three deer hunters in the Rogue River National Forest in Oregon were ambushed by cannabis growers, and one was wounded. In Hawaii, it is speculated that a couple who were murdered in a remote national forest were victims of these outlaw cultivators.

Trying to Control Cultivation and Distribution

Marijuana was first brought under federal control by the Marijuana Tax Act of 1937. This act prohibited cultivation, possession, and distribution of hemp plants, except for those grown for the manufacture of rope, twine, and other coarse woven products. Since that time, the severity of antimarijuana laws has varied; whereas the legislation passed in the 1950s ordered mandatory punishment for users, the laws were reformed in the 1960s and 1970s to emphasize medical treatment for drug addicts. The 1980s have seen a return to more stringent legislation against the possession and sale of marijuana.

The DEA is attempting to control what is still a prosperous illegal drug trade by destroying marijuana at the source. With the cooperation of law enforcement agencies in Mexico, Colombia, Peru, and other major exporters of marijuana, the DEA is seizing and destroying marijuana crops. In one sweep during 1986, 9,000 metric tons of marijuana, with a street value of about $4 billion, were destroyed in raids on five plantations in Chihuahua, a state in northern Mexico.

Not all of the antidrug raids have been as successful. One clandestine antidrug operation known as "Hat Trick" called for Colombian soldiers to raid marijuana plantations in the Guajira Peninsula between the Gulf of Venezuela and the Caribbean. With Panamanian and Venezuelan soldiers sealing off their borders as smuggling routes, the traffickers would be forced to send the marijuana by sea, where it would be intercepted by U.S. Coast Guard and Navy vessels. Word of "Hat Trick" leaked out to the press, and only small amounts of marijuana were seized.

In addition, marijuana traffickers have not hesitated to use violence against drug enforcement agents. In Mexico in November 1985, for example, 17 policemen surprised 50 traffickers in the act of loading a boat with 1,300 pounds of marijuana. The smugglers returned the fire, and when the shoot-out ended, all 17 agents were dead.

Fighting Marijuana on the Home Front

In August 1985, the U.S. Department of Justice launched a nationwide campaign to eradicate the domestic cannabis crop. The plan called for federal, state, and local officials to work together to destroy millions of cannabis plants in 50 states. In the first months of the campaign, 362,000 plants — one-fifth of the U.S. marijuana crop—were uprooted.

Ten years earlier, marijuana eradication programs conducted by the DEA had come under intense criticism for one of the methods employed — aerial spraying of the fields with the weed killer *paraquat*. The first operation employing pa-

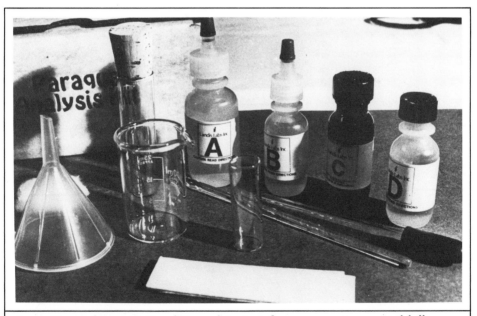

A marijuana home testing kit used to test for paraquat, a weed killer. Early marijuana eradication programs conducted by the DEA included the spraying of paraquat, which can be lethal to humans even in small doses.

In Lebanon, Bedouins haul in the day's harvest of hashish. Hashish has a THC content of 10 to 15% and has much stronger effects than marijuana.

raquat took place over cannabis patches in the Chattahoochee National Forest in Georgia. This was followed by helicopter sprayings of cannabis in the mountains of Kentucky and Tennessee.

Before the first week of spraying was over, the program was attacked by residents of the area involved, as well as by local officials and environmental groups. Opposition to paraquat spraying was based primarily on the fact that paraquat can be lethal to humans if swallowed — in doses as small as one-tenth of an ounce — and can cause serious lung scarring if inhaled.

Four hundred persons living near the Chattahoochee National Forest won a temporary restraining order barring further spraying in the area. A similar motion filed by Kentuckians living near the Daniel Boone National Forest, where spraying was also being conducted, was turned down. However, opposition to the spraying continued to grow.

Many states opposed paraquat spraying, stating that the herbicide was doing more harm than good. For example, paraquat that was sprayed on cannabis would sometimes drift, contaminating other crops and livestock. So widespread has been the opposition to the spraying that the DEA has stopped using the herbicide, not only domestically but in Mexico as well.

Hashish: A More Potent Product of Cannabis

Hashish is the pure resin obtained from the cannabis plants cultivated in Asian countries. The resin is extracted from the flowering tops of the plants by beating the tops against burlap. A dark brown substance results, to which sugar is often added for weight.

Whereas most street marijuana contains less than 1 to 3% THC, hashish has a THC concentration of 10 to 15%. Consequently, the effects of hashish are stronger than those produced by marijuana. Often hashish will cause the user to enter a dreamlike state, experiencing profound distortions in the sense of time and space. Sometimes anxiety and panic occur; more often there is a feeling of euphoria. Apathy, a deterioration of mental processes, and bizarre behavior are frequently observed in habitual users.

Hashish is the product of the cannabis plant most commonly used in western Europe, and it has been gaining in popularity in the United States since the 1960s. In 1983, it was estimated that 150 metric tons of hashish were smuggled into the United States. Reports of greatly increased hashish trafficking activity indicate that the figure is much higher today.

Most of the hashish that comes into the United States is produced in Lebanon, Pakistan, and Afghanistan. Morocco is an important producer of hashish but most of its production is consumed in that country or sent to Europe. Nepal and India produce small amounts of the drug, but primarily for domestic consumption.

Because government officials have increased drug curtailment activity in the Mediterranean sea, it is becoming more difficult for growers in the major hashish-exporting countries to export their wares to North America. Some of this hashish is routed from Pakistan through Southeast Asia and via the Pacific Ocean to the West Coast of the United States. But this route is becoming more hazardous as well because antidrug teams are cracking down on these illegal trafficking procedures.

A poppy flower and bud. When the poppy is harvested, its unripened seed pod is lanced to release the milky sap inside. This sap is opium. Nearly 3,000 poppies are needed to produce 1.6 kilograms of opium.

CHAPTER 3

PRODUCTS OF THE POPPY: OPIUM, MORPHINE, AND HEROIN

The poppy, or *Papaver somniferum*, is a pretty flower with petals of white, red, mauve, or purple. It is also the source of opium, which, along with its *narcotic derivatives* (drugs such as heroin and morphine that are opium based), has been used for its painkilling properties — and abused for its euphoric ones—since prehistoric times.

Opiates act primarily on the central nervous system, the eyes, the respiratory system, and the gastrointestinal tract. More specifically, experts believe that the drugs produce their effects by mimicking the body's natural opiates and interacting with specific receptors in the brain that are designed to receive the natural opiates. The effects of narcotics are diverse, ranging from pain relief and euphoria to — in the case of overdose — mental confusion, nausea and vomiting, and death.

Opiates are tremendously addictive. A person taking a narcotic to experience an analgesic or euphoric effect may begin to crave the drug, both psychologically and physically. At this time, the user's tolerance builds up and the person invariably discovers that he or she must take the drug in larger and larger doses in order to experience the same effect.

Algerian Harem *by Eugène Delacroix. By the 7th century C.E., many Islamic cultures had discovered that opium's effects were intensified if it was smoked through a pipe like the one shown here.*

Once a person becomes addicted, stopping use of the drug causes unpleasant withdrawal symptoms, such as nausea, sleeplessness, depression, and hallucinations.

The History of Opiate Use

Opium was first used around 4000 B.C.E. in ancient Sumeria (present-day Near East), probably for medicinal purposes. The opium was collected by slashing open poppy pods and then drying the milky juice that seeped out. The ancient Greeks discovered the euphoric properties of the drug and were probably among the first to use narcotics regularly for recreational purposes. The Greeks and ancient Romans also depended on opium for its pain-relieving properties; the 5th-century Greek physician Hippocrates cited the therapeutic powers of opium, and three centuries later Galen, a Greek physician practicing in the Roman Empire, treated his patients — many of whom were gladiators — with a narcotic opium preparation called *mithridate*.

By the 7th century C.E., opium had become a popular drug in the Turkish and Islamic cultures of western Asia, which discovered that the effects of the narcotic were much stronger if it was smoked rather than eaten. The drug was also becoming widespread in India and China, where it was used mainly for medicinal purposes. In the 16th century, the Swiss physician Paracelsus concocted an opium-based medicine called laudanum, which he claimed could cure any painful disease. It was not until 200 years later, however, when the British opened trade routes to India, that opium became widely available in Europe.

An opium den in New York City's Chinatown in 1925. After recreational opium use was introduced in the United States in the late 19th century, opium dens became popular haunts for many addicts.

Opium was phenomenonally popular in Great Britain during the 19th century and continued to thrive in Asia. Addiction became so widespread in China, in fact, that the Chinese government attempted to ban its production. However, the British, who were conducting a profitable opium trade in Asia, opposed the ban and between 1839 and 1842 fought a series of battles called the Opium Wars to force China to legalize opium.

Opium in the United States

Opium was introduced to the United States in the early 19th century for medicinal purposes — to relieve pain, suppress coughing, act as a sedative, and relieve diarrhea. Then, in the 1850s and 1860s, Chinese workers who immigrated to the United States introduced the practice of opium smoking. Thousands of Americans became addicted. Opium use was widespread and legal until it was placed under federal regulation by the Harrison Narcotics Act of 1914. Today, opium plays only a small role in the U.S. illicit drug traffic, because drug dealers can make far greater profit by converting raw opium into heroin.

Morphine

In 1802, the German pharmacist Friederich Serturner isolated the principal alkaloid of opium. The new derivative, which Serturner called morphine — after Morpheus, the Greek god of sleep and dreams — was one of the most important medical discoveries of the 19th century.

Morphine could relieve almost any kind of pain, and, when injected by the newly developed hypodermic syringe, it could do so quickly. During the Civil War, soldiers were given supplies of morphine along with hypodermic syringes to ease the pain of battle wounds and the symptoms of dysentery, an intestinal disorder. During the mid-19th century, morphine was freely available to the public — at the local drug store or through the mail — in powder, tablet, or liquid form.

It was not until several decades after the Civil War that the medical profession became aware that morphine was addictive. By that time an estimated 400,000 people — or 2% of the population—were suffering from morphine addiction.

Today morphine is legally available only as a highly restricted prescription drug. It is still valued as an analgesic, one that often relieves pain when nothing else will, but is prescribed only in hospitals, and only in extreme cases. Because most opiate addicts are users of the more potent and shorter-acting heroin, morphine does not figure significantly in the illicit drug trade. Most morphine addicts in the 1980s are members of the medical profession and hospital personnel who have access to the drug.

Heroin

Heroin, which is a semisynthetic derivative of opium, is produced by the action of a chemical called *acetylchloride* on morphine. This procedure can be performed with simple laboratory equipment costing less than a thousand dollars. The result is an odorless, crystalline white powder with a bitter taste.

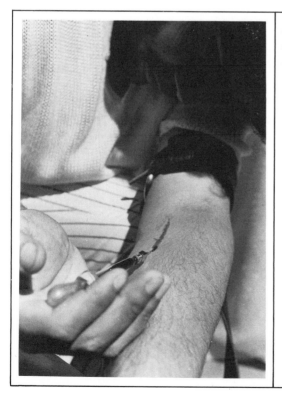

Heroin is usually injected by the addict, for quick absorption into the bloodstream.

A young Thai farmer lances an opium poppy. After the raw opium is collected, it is sold for further processing at primitive factories called opium and alkaloid works.

Ironically, when heroin was introduced in 1898 it was hailed not only as a nonaddictive alternative to morphine but as a cure for morphine addiction. Several years passed before it was discovered that heroin was as addictive as morphine and even more dangerous.

Specifically, heroin is three times more potent than morphine. Its smaller bulk makes it easier to smuggle and much more profitable for dealers and pushers. Heroin is generally taken by injection, which adds an additional danger to its use. The sharing of needles, which is so common among addicts, can spread such dangerous diseases as septicemia, infectious hepatitis, and AIDS.

Moreover, pure heroin is never sold to the addict. By the time it reaches the user, it has been diluted 20 to 100 times with quinine, talcum powder, epsom salts, soap powder, milk sugar, baking soda, or some other dilutant. It has been speculated that quinine used for this purpose may be responsible for some of the deaths attributed to heroin.

Despite the obvious dangers of heroin, there remains an astonishing number of heroin addicts in the United States. A 1981 study estimated that there were 490,000 heroin users in the nation, and it is believed that the number has increased since then.

Gathering Opium from the Poppy

The world's biggest grower of opium poppies is India; opium for medicinal purposes is one of this nation's major exports. Producing opium is legal in India, provided that the growers — most of whom are peasant families — are licensed. The Indian government can therefore collect taxes on the opium and prevent the drug from being diverted to the illicit drug trade. The government has granted opium-growing licenses to approximately 170,000 peasant families in India, and about a million people are involved in the labor-intensive work of producing the drug.

As it grows, the opium poppy produces alkaloids and stores them in its cells. These alkaloids concentrate as a milky sap in the seed capsules. This sap is opium. When the poppy is harvested, its unripened seed pod is lanced to release the alkaloid-rich sap, which starts to dry as it runs down the pod. Within 24 hours, the sap, now dark and hardened, is scraped off with an iron scoop.

Although a seed pod can be lanced several times to yield opium, the amount forthcoming is minuscule. Nearly 3,000 poppies are needed to produce a *joi*—1.6 kilograms (3.5 pounds)—of opium.

After the raw opium is collected, it is sold for further processing at primitive factories called opium and alkaloid works. Here the raw opium is placed in rectangular pans that sit in the sun. Periodically, the opium is stirred by hand with wooden paddles. The purpose is to reduce the amount of water content in the raw opium from about 30% to 10% or less. At the end of each day the workers at these factories are often covered with opium and must scrape the precious juice off their bodies so that it can be collected.

The Golden Triangle

Very little of the heroin consumed in the United States is smuggled from India; 20% of it comes from poppies grown in three southwestern Asian countries — Burma, Thailand, and Laos—known together as the Golden Triangle.

Poppies in these countries are grown in mountainous areas. After the poppies are harvested and the raw opium extracted, the opium is taken in caravans of pack mules to laboratories for processing into morphine base or heroin.

Much of the opium trade in these countries is carried out by two groups. One is the Burmese Communist Party (BCP), which controls territory near the Burma/Thailand border. The other is the Shan United Army (SUA), another insurgent force that does not recognize the authority of the Burmese government. Both of these groups have laboratories along the Burma/Thailand border. Their refineries are not in continuous production, because they must depend on the availability of raw materials and because of the fluctuating demand for heroin. During occasional government antidrug campaigns, the organizations must suspend operations and go underground temporarily.

The Golden Crescent and Mexico

Estimates of opium production in 1986 in the southwestern Asian countries of Afghanistan, Iran, and Pakistan — known as the Golden Crescent—ranged from 740 to 1,060 metric tons.

Afghanistan, which alone supplied almost 50% of the entire Golden Crescent opium production in 1986, has laboratory facilities that convert the opium to heroin. Most of these facilities are in the eastern and southwestern regions of the country. Some of the newly derived heroin is then smuggled into Pakistan, and some goes to Iran, which is itself a large producer of opium (200 to 400 metric tons in 1986).

Mexico also produces a formidable amount of opium. Although this country's poppy crop (an estimated 21 metric tons in 1984) is not as large as those of the Golden Triangle or Golden Crescent countries, it is growing rapidly. In 1984, 40% more land was devoted to poppy cultivation than during the previous year, and according to a U.S. government estimate, one-third of the heroin entering the United States comes from Mexico.

A Mexican federal agent kicks in the door of an illegal heroin lab. It is estimated that nearly one-third of all the heroin entering the United States comes from Mexico.

Smuggling Routes

Smuggling routes are constantly changing. As a law enforcement crackdown closes one route, another opens. At present, most heroin produced in the Golden Triangle countries is funneled through Thailand for transshipment abroad, although other routes have been developed in response to stepped-up operations by Burmese and Thai police. In addition, shutdowns of refineries near the Burma/Thailand border by military units have led to the rerouting of much of the Golden Triangle opium traffic south through Burma to Malaysia, where many refineries are now located. As a result, Malaysia has become an important transshipper of Golden Triangle heroin.

Iran is an important outlet for opium, morphine base, and heroin produced in the Golden Crescent countries. Much of the opium transshipped to Iran is then smuggled to Turkey, which, because of its location between the opium-producing areas in Pakistan and Afghanistan and the consuming countries in western Europe and the United States, is a logical "conveyer belt" for illicit drugs.

One of the smuggling routes from Turkey leads to Syria, where heroin is shipped by air to western Europe or the United States through Damascus Airport or in small vessels through the Mediterranean. Another major route is overland from Turkey by way of eastern Europe. Turkey also has laboratories in which morphine base and opium gum are sometimes converted to heroin before being shipped out of the country.

Illicit production of heroin is minimal in India. However, that country serves as both a market and transshipment center for opium from Afghanistan and Pakistan, and for heroin from the Golden Triangle countries. Most Mexican heroin is smuggled into the United States by cars, trucks, buses, and pedestrians. Some of it is transported by small private aircraft.

International Efforts to Control the Opium Trade

The governments of both Burma and Thailand are trying to curb the flow of opiates from the Golden Triangle. In 1984, the Thai government began a program to destroy heroin re-

Ayatollah Khomeini of Iran addresses foreign guests at a celebration marking the anniversary of the Iranian revolution. Iran is a large producer of opium and an important outlet for many of the opiates produced in the other Golden Crescent countries.

fineries, cut off the smuggling routes to Burma, and eradicate the poppy crops in Thailand. The Burmese government has concentrated on poppy eradication, using planes to spray the fields with plant killers. The government is also attempting to stop the activities of the BCP, the SUA, and others involved in opiate trafficking. As a result of its program, Thailand has been able to reduce its poppy cultivation drastically; cultivation declined from about 9,000 hectares in 1985 to fewer than 5,000 hectares the following year. The government of Burma, however, has been less successful, and the government of Laos does not yet have a program to halt opium production.

The government of Pakistan is attempting to reduce the opium poppy crop in its northwest frontier province. It is assisted in this mission by outside agencies, including the United Nations Fund for Drug Abuse Control, which provides monetary incentives for farmers to switch to other crops. Despite these efforts, there is still enough opium available, including that grown in Afghanistan, to provide raw materials for the heroin refineries in the area.

Although the drug crackdown programs were moderately successful in the early 1980s, production of opium increased once again in 1986. Many factors appear to be responsible for this increase, most notable of which are the higher prices for opium brought about by increasing demand and the Pakistani government's apparent inability to enforce its control policies adequately.

Although the government of Afghanistan has taken few active measures to control opium production, there has been a drop in poppy cultivation there since 1979, the year military occupation by the Soviet Union began. In 1984 the government of Iran instituted severe measures, including the death penalty, against drug traffickers.

As a result of anti–drug trafficking efforts by the Turkish government, some of the opiates from southwestern Asia that were formerly trafficked through Turkey have been rerouted to Syria and Lebanon. However, Turkey continues to be a major conduit for these drugs.

The Mexican Attorney General's office has its own air fleet of planes and helicopters, which conducts a poppy eradication program using herbicides. This program is augmented

A Mexican helicopter ranger lands in a field planted with marijuana and opium. The Mexican attorney general's office has its own fleet of planes and helicopters that spray herbicides as part of a poppy eradication program.

on the ground by the Mexican army. Sweep operations are concentrated in the key poppy-growing and opium-producing states of Oaxaca, Guerrero, and Chihuahua.

Fighting Opium in the United States

U.S. influence in the Golden Triangle is restricted to Thailand and those parts of Burma that are under the control of the central government, because there are strained relations between the governments of the United States and Laos. Therefore, the United States is concentrating its efforts to curtail drug trafficking along the Thai/Burma border, in the interior of Thailand, and in the Shan province of Burma. It is also working for the eradication of opium and heroin production in these two countries.

Thailand is a major focus of U.S. efforts in this region, because it is not only the major producer of opium but also the transshipment center for virtually all of the Golden Triangle's heroin. The U.S. anti-opium program in Thailand consists of crop control, police and customs interdiction assistance, and financial support for the Association of Southeastern Asian Nations' own antidrug program.

As in the Golden Triangle, strained diplomatic relations between the United States and, in this case, both Iran and Afghanistan have severely limited American antidrug operations in the Golden Crescent. The U.S. strategy in southwestern Asia, therefore, is to support programs in Pakistan and Turkey. The emphasis in Pakistan is on eradicating the poppy crop in the northwest frontier province. As mentioned above, the United Nations Fund for Drug Abuse Control contributes to a program assisting farmers who stop cultivating poppies to find an alternate source of income. Another goal of American antidrug strategy is to control the illicit opium and heroin traffic in this area.

Mexico is the largest single-country supplier to the United States of both heroin and marijuana, and the U.S. government therefore puts a great deal of diplomatic pressure on the Mexican government to control both poppy and marijuana production within its borders. The Mexican government has created eradication programs, but they have not been particularly successful. For example, it is estimated that poppy production in Mexico increased by 25% during 1986. Nonetheless, the two governments continue to cooperate in law enforcement efforts to curtail production and distribution of illicit substances.

An Egyptian sculpture of a peasant making beer, dating from about 2000 B.C.E. Alcohol is the world's oldest psychoactive drug and has a history as rich and varied as civilization itself.

CHAPTER 4

ALCOHOL

Alcohol is the world's oldest, and America's most popular, psychoactive drug. Its history is intertwined with that of civilization, and its abuse is one of the major problems of modern society. Technically, alcohol belongs to a family of chemicals that contains carbon and hydrogen atoms. There are several different kinds of alcohol, all but one of which are highly poisonous. The one exception is ethanol or ethyl alcohol, which is the form of alcohol found in alcoholic beverages.

The Effects of Alcohol

When ingested in moderate quantities, alcohol creates a sense of well-being and relaxation. This is the effect that attracts so many people to drinking. However, alcohol is a central nervous system depressant, and when taken in larger quantities, it can interfere with voluntary motor functions, such as speaking and walking. At even higher doses, alcohol can depress the entire motor area of the brain, an action that causes serious emotional and behavioral problems. For example, an intoxicated drinker may experience crying or laughing jags or become belligerent or maudlin. When the alcohol level in the blood reaches .25%, the body's immune system is impaired and white cells are severely reduced, an effect similar to that seen in a person in shock. Concentrations of .40% to .50% lead to coma. Higher levels than that affect the lower brain, where breathing and heartbeat are regulated, and can be fatal.

The History of Alcohol

Prehistoric humans probably first discovered alcoholic beverages when they tasted the juice that came from fermented sugar-containing fruits, berries, and grains. (Fermentation is a natural chemical process whereby sugar is converted to carbon dioxide and alcohol by the action of yeast.) The alcoholic content of these beverages was no higher than 12%, because fermentation stops at that point. Alcohol was the most widespread drug in ancient Asia, Europe, and Africa. There is evidence that people were drinking alcoholic beverages in China as far back as 2285 B.C.E., and in Egypt as early as 2000 B.C.E. Wine was an essential part of the ancient Greek and Roman cultures.

Beer was first discovered in ancient times, and it became a popular drink during the Middle Ages. There are medieval accounts of drunken feasts and ensuing brawls and records of thousands of gallons of beer and ale being consumed. During the same period, the wine distillation process was perfected by monks in monasteries, who cultivated extensive church vineyards that produced far more wine than was needed for religious purposes.

Consumption of whiskey and gin became widespread in Europe during the 16th and 17th centuries. Both beverages were used initially for medicinal purposes, and both became widely abused. Gin, which was brought to England from Holland, was even given in lieu of wages to some of England's poor workers during the Industrial Revolution in the 1700s and 1800s.

Alcohol in America

The history of alcohol in the United States is really a story of an ongoing battle between forces for and against prohibition. During the colonial era, Scotch-Irish settlers in western Pennsylvania had begun making whiskey when they found that it was enormously more profitable to turn their rye and corn harvests into a liquid form than to sell them as food. In fact, consumption of alcohol, particularly of beer and ale, was routine during the colonial era. But by the 1800s, anti-alcohol sentiments were running high in the United States. In 1845, Maine passed a statewide alcohol prohibition act and by 1865, 13 states had followed suit.

The temperance movement grew in strength because excessive drinking began to be perceived as a major national problem. The consequences of alcohol abuse were most apparent in urban areas, where millions of newly arrived immigrant men drank to forget the brutal hours they worked and the squalor of their living conditions in the slums. The

An illuminated medieval manuscript page from Les Tres Riches Heures du Duc de Berry *depicting a September grape harvest. During the Middle Ages the wine distillation process was perfected by monks who cultivated church vineyards.*

The Women's Christian Temperance Union *by Ben Shahn. The WCTU was instrumental in the passing of the Prohibition amendment.*

wives of these men — complaining that their husbands often spent their paychecks in the local saloon and observing how excessive drinking tended to brutalize the men — were a driving force behind the temperance movement. In 1874, they helped found the Women's Christian Temperance Union (WCTU).

By the time the United States entered World War I in 1917, the drive toward national prohibition was well underway. As a result of the lobbying efforts of the WCTU and other temperance organizations, 25 states had already passed dry laws. Soon, a constitutional amendment to ban the manufacture, sale, and consumption of alcoholic beverages was circulating among the states for ratification. On January 16, 1919, the 36th state approved the amendment, and Prohibition became the law of the land.

Prohibition: An Experiment That Failed

From the start, Prohibition was doomed to failure, for there was no national will to accept it. The criminal element soon discovered that bootlegging liquor to an eager market was a lucrative source of illegal income. Fleets of small boats brought a steady stream of rum and other bootleg liquors from Cuba to Florida and the Gulf states. Ships loaded with wines and liquors from Europe anchored off the U.S. coasts while motor launches ran the contraband ashore. Other bootleg liquor was smuggled in across the Mexican and Canadian borders. The bootleg trade was controlled in the United States by organized crime syndicates, led by such mobsters as Al Capone and George "Bugs" Moran, many of whom were in league with corrupt officials.

"Speakeasies," or illegal bars, soon sprang up and became popular places for both women and men. In fact, one of the social effects of prohibition was a breakdown of sex barriers when it came to imbibing alcohol. National drinking habits changed in other ways, as more and more Americans who had been beer drinkers before prohibition discovered hard liquor and the various cocktails that could be mixed using these beverages as a base.

It was apparent by the late 1920s that prohibition had failed. There were now more speakeasies than there ever were saloons, and alcohol consumption had not declined

A Fourth of July anti-Prohibition parade in New York City during the 1920s. Never particularly popular or successful, Prohibition was repealed by the 21st Amendment in 1933.

It is estimated that more than half of the nation's 6 million young drinkers have serious problems with alcohol.

significantly. National politicians were not blind to this fact and began to campaign for a repeal. Finally, in 1933, a newly elected Congress passed the 21st Amendment to repeal prohibition. The amendment was promptly ratified by a sufficient number of states to become law.

Alcohol Consumption Today

Almost half of the people in the United States today drink alcoholic beverages. This has become a matter of national concern primarily because of two problems: alcoholism and drunken driving.

Alcoholism, now recognized as a medical problem, is estimated to affect more than 10 million Americans. An increasing number of counseling services and treatment centers have been established to deal with alcoholism in the schools, in the workplace, and in the home. Driving under the influence of alcohol is a major problem among those under the age of 25. Each year, 9,500 Americans in this age bracket die in alcohol-related highway accidents. In response to this statistic, Congress passed a law in 1986 that encouraged states to raise the drinking age to 21. Under the terms of the act, states that allow drinking by persons younger than 21 would lose 5% of their federal highway funds in 1987 and 10% in 1988. By late 1987, 28 states had passed the desired law.

Despite a growing awareness that alcohol is a mind-altering and potentially dangerous drug, the fact remains that most people who drink it do so in moderation and with little ill effect. For people who do not develop drinking problems, wine and liquor remain what they have always been — social lubricants that enhance a range of social events, from weddings and other celebrations to fine meals.

Wine Production

Winemaking is a complicated process that differs according to the desired color and flavor of the wine and also according to the region. Although the basic procedures are outlined below, intermediate steps are sometimes taken, depending on the type of wine being produced.

Most wines are produced from grapes, although some are made from other fruits. Proper harvesting is crucial to producing a good wine. The grapes must be picked at just the right stage of ripening and they must be kept as cool as possible until they arrive at the winery, where they are de-stemmed and crushed. Sulfur dioxide is then added to the juice to prevent the growth of undesirable microorganisms. If white wine is being produced, the juice is separated from the solid material of the grape. For red wine, the separation of the juice from the solids takes place later, during fermentation.

The fermentation process is the most important part of wine production. Natural wines, called table wines, are produced by fermenting the grape juice through exposure to minute fungi called yeasts; fermentation is simply the conversion of the grape sugar to ethyl alcohol. Once this process takes place, the alcohol content of the wine is about 12%. One class of natural wines, called sparkling wines, undergoes a second fermentation; this results in a higher alcohol content and an excess of carbon dioxide, which causes the beverage to "bubble," or become carbonated. Dessert and appetizer wines, such as sherry, are sweeter than table wines. They are also more potent than both table wines and sparkling wines because extra alcohol is added during the fermentation process.

Following fermentation, the wine is put through a special procedure called "racking." During this phase the yeast cells and other sediments that gather at the bottom of the wine are collected and then siphoned off. Then comes the aging of the wine in white oak barrels or casks or in redwood tanks. The porosity of the wood allows a limited amount of oxygen to seep in, which is desirable; the wood of the container also contributes to the flavor of the wine. The final phase of wine production is bottling. Sometimes wine is pasteurized or filtered before being sealed in the bottle. This last step is a form of sterilization.

A French family enjoys a hearty lunch accompanied by wine. For economic and historic reasons wine is the most popular beverage in the country.

The October grape harvest in the Champagne district of France. Champagne, famous for its sparkling wines, is one of the most important wine-producing regions of France.

The Wines of France

France is the world's major wine-producing country. This is not because of the quantity of its production — Italy produces more — but because of the quality. France produces more kinds of wines than any other country and has turned the appreciation of fine wines into an art and their production almost into a science.

To maintain the quality of the country's fine wines, the French government regulates their production. The law fixes the geographical boundaries of the vineyards to assure that wines bearing the name of a region are actually produced in that region. The law also sets the maximum quantity of quality wine each vineyard may produce of a given vintage, or season. Wines produced under these controls are entitled to bear the phrase *Appelation Controlée* on the label, a French government guarantee of quality.

The most important wine-producing regions of France are Bordeaux, which produces red clarets and sweet white wines; Burgundy, best known for its sparkling white, red, and rosé wines as well as its rich red and white wines; Champagne, the most famous producer of sparkling wines; and the Rhône Valley, known for its wines with a deep red color, which are at their best after a long aging process — a minimum of 12 to 15 years. Other regions in France noted for their quality wines include the château country of the Loire Valley in central France; the Côtes de Provence along the Mediterranean coast; Languedoc, a province on the southeastern coast of France; and Jura, a province near the Swiss border.

The Wines of Italy

Viticulture, or the production of wines, has been a major industry in Italy since the time of the Romans. Until recently, however, the industry was not carefully regulated, as it has been in France, to assure the maintenance of quality. Because

A worker stomps grapes in the small Italian town of Monte Porzio. Though grapes have traditionally been crushed by foot, modern machinery is now usually used to extract the juice from the grapes.

the climate was so ideal for the growing of grapes, the Italian vintners were often content to let nature take its course and allowed the vines to grow untended — without much pruning and without much thought as to which grapes would grow best in specific regions.

That situation began to change in 1963, when the Italian Wine Law was passed. The law specified the types of wines that must be produced in given areas and also set up a system in which wines would be graded according to newly established standards of quality.

Perhaps the best known of the Italian wines is Chianti, which is produced in the Chianti mountain range in Tuscany, in central Italy. Because Chianti contains a substantial amount of bitartrates, which are acidic additives, it is a rough, harsh, full-bodied wine. Its roughness makes Chianti an ideal wine to eat with well-seasoned, oily foods, and its tartness makes these foods easier to digest. Other famous Italian wines are Asti Spumante, which comes from Asti, a hill town in the northern Alpine region; Soave, produced in the city of the same name in the province of Venetia; vermouth, produced primarily in Turin; and marsala, a sweet, dark wine made in Sicily.

Other European Wines

Like France and Italy, Germany has a law controlling the quality and production of its wines. Under this law wines must be produced from approved grape varieties grown in Germany, and the name of the bottler must appear on the label.

The most famous wine-producing areas in Germany are along the Rhine River, which is where the variety of blended wines known as Liebfraumilch wines are made, as well as Moselle wines, known for their light fruitiness and tingling sharpness. West Germany is also the world's largest producer and exporter of sparkling wines. Unlike French wines, German wines do not age well and should be consumed soon after purchase.

The best-known wine made in Portugal is port, a blend of many wines. There are two main varieties of port — ruby port, which is used as a dessert wine, and tawny port, which is low in sugar content and is therefore considered an aperitif

A bottling line at a California winery. California is the most important wine-producing area in the United States, with more than 700 square miles of vineyards producing wines of consistent quality.

or appetizer wine. Spain's best-known wines, port and sherry, are produced in Jerez de la Frontera in Andalucia, the southernmost region of the country. Both wines are popular export items in England and the rest of western Europe, as well as in the United States.

American Wines

Wines have been produced in the eastern part of the United States since colonial days, particularly in areas of New York, Ohio, New Jersey, Virginia, Missouri, and Michigan. The most significant of these areas is the Finger Lakes region of upper New York State. All types of wine are produced, but the region is best known for its sparkling wines. Indeed, one such wine, produced at Hammondsport, at the lower end of Lake Keuka, won a gold medal at the Paris Exposition of 1867. Sherry made from Niagara, Concord, and Dutchess grapes is also a popular product of the Finger Lake wineries.

But the most important wine-producing area in the United States is the state of California. The climate, soil, and general conditions of almost every wine-growing region in the world can be duplicated in this state, and there are more than 700 square miles of vineyard there, growing every important variety of European grape. There are ten important wine growing areas in California. Most of their districts are in the San Francisco Bay area or farther north, in the Sonoma and Napa valleys. Unlike Europe, where each district specializes in one type of wine, most wine types are produced in every district, and some wines are blends of products from several districts. What is lost as a result is the individuality of each vintage found in Europe. What is gained is continuity and consistent quality.

Brandy and Liqueurs

Brandy is an alcoholic beverage made from the distillation of wine or a fermented mash of fruit. The distillation process simply eliminates the water from the wine, leaving its spirit or "soul." Although brandies can be produced in any part of the world where grapes or other fruits are grown, the finest, cognac and Armagnac, are both distilled from grapes grown in western France. Most American brandies are produced in

A cognac distillery in France. Cognac and Armagnac, the world's finest brandies, are both distilled from grapes grown in western France.

California from grapes grown in that state; brandies are also produced from fruits such as apples, apricots, and plums.

Liqueurs, also called cordials, are produced by combining distilled spirits such as brandy, gin, rum, or whiskey with flavoring agents, usually a sugar syrup of a particular flavor. The result is a very sweet, potent drink. Because liqueurs also contain essential oils that tend to aid digestion, they are served primarily as after-dinner drinks.

Liqueurs can have as their flavoring agent a wide variety of fruits, plants, and herbs, and can therefore be produced in virtually every part of the world. A few liqueurs that are distinctive products of their country are ouzo, an anise-flavored liqueur made in Greece and Cyprus; Benedictine, which originated in a Benedictine abbey in Fécamp, France, and is one of the oldest liqueurs in the world; Marnique, an Australian liqueur made from Australian brandy and tangerines; Wishniak, a Polish liqueur made from cherries and spices; and Kahlua, a coffee-flavored liqueur from Mexico.

Beer

Beer is not only one type of malt beverage but also the general name for lager, ale, malt liquor, stout, porter, and bock beer — all of which are produced by fermenting a cereal brew and malt. (Malt is produced when kernels of grain — usually barley — are steeped in warm water until they sprout and then dried in a kiln.) The ingredients are virtually the same for all beers. Usually malted barley forms the base, although sometimes other starchy cereal grains are used. The other ingedients are water, hops (the dried, ripe cones from the flowers of the humulus plant) and yeast.

The first step in brewing beer is to prepare cereal mash by grinding the malt to a coarse grist and adding water. Other cereals are then mixed in, and the mash is cooked to liquefy the starch. The malt's enzymes break down the proteins and convert the starches to fermentable sugars, maltose, and dextrin. The liquid that results, called the wort, is filtered, then boiled in brew kettles. Additional hops are added during the process to provide extra flavor.

After this initial step, yeast is added and the hops are removed. The liquid is then left to ferment for about a week. Next, the beer is aged for several months in tanks at near-

Beer fermenting in a large wooden vat. After fermentation, the beer is aged in tanks for several months at near-freezing temperatures before it is carbonated, filtered, bottled, and shipped out for consumption.

freezing temperatures to permit mellowing and sedimentation. When the aging is completed, the beer is carbonated and goes through a final filtering. Barreled or draft beer is then shipped out for quick consumption. Canned and bottled beer is first pasteurized.

The most common beer in the United States is the light-bodied, lightly flavored brew called lager that is generally drunk chilled. Malt liquor is a beer with a higher alcoholic content, often with hops added in the brewing process. Ale is a golden-colored brew with a slightly higher alcoholic content than beer. Stout is a darker ale with a sweeter, somewhat bitter flavor and with more hops added. Porter is an ale even darker than stout and has a rich creamy head. Bock beer, a darker, sweeter, more full-bodied beer, is brewed in the winter for use in the spring.

Beer is brewed in just about every area of the United States, although a great deal of it is produced in such midwestern states as Missouri and Wisconsin. Although the United States is the world's largest producer of malt beverages (100 million barrels annually, each barrel containing 31 gallons), it ranks 10th — behind several European nations — in consuming them (16 gallons per person per year).

The most popular European beers in the United States are the light Pilsner beers of Czechoslovakia and the German, Danish, and Dutch lagers. All of these are golden-hued and fresh-tasting. Less to the American taste but becoming more popular are the ales and stout of England and Ireland. The United States also imports beer from its neighbors to the north and south; Canadian ales are becoming extremely popular in America, as are the light, delicate beers of Mexico. In addition, Kirin and Tsingtao, distinctive beers from, respectively, Japan and China, have become popular in America.

Liquor

Like beer, liquor is made from a mash of grain mixed with malt and yeast. After the mash is fermented, a kind of "beer" is brewed, which is then heated as a first step in the process of distillation. A comparatively modern process developed only a few hundred years ago, distillation is what makes liquor a more potent beverage than beer.

When the "beer" is heated, the water is boiled off, and the alcohol vapors, which have a higher boiling point than water, are caught. This part of the process is repeated as often as needed to create a liquid with a much higher alcoholic content. The alcoholic content of a beverage is measured by "proof." Straight alcohol is 200 proof, which means that a beverage with 50% alcohol would be 100 proof, 25% alcohol would be 50 proof, etc.

There are several types of distilled liquor, which differ according to the type of grain in the mash. Whiskies include bourbon, which is made only in Kentucky and is prepared from a mash that contains at least 51% corn. Rye, a whiskey made in the United States and Canada, must contain at least 51% rye grain in its mash. Scotch is a whiskey made in Scotland that contains a mixed mash of cereals, including maize. Irish whiskey is made in Northern Ireland from mash that contains malted barley. In the Republic of Ireland a variety of grains are used. Irish whiskey is distilled in huge pot stills and, like Scotch and bourbon, is aged for a long period of time. Irish whiskey must in fact be at least seven years old to be exported.

Rum, vodka, and gin are the other major distilled liquors. Rum is made from the fermented juice of the sugar cane or from fermented molasses or mixtures of these. Rum can be either dark or light, full-bodied or light-bodied, depending on the methods used in its distillation. Rum is produced in New England, the West Indies, South America, Cuba, Puerto Rico, the Virgin Islands, Haiti, Martinique, and Barbados. Vodka is a mixture of alcohol and water, with no additional flavorings. It is distilled from different grains and, in northern Europe, from potatoes. This distillate is further refined by being passed through layers of charcoal. Gin is a mixture of pure alcohol, pure water, and flavoring. The alcohol-water mixture is derived from the distillation of a fermented grain mash, which is redistilled with the alcohol vapors passed over certain flavoring ingredients. The most common flavoring agent is the juniper berry. However, other ingedients are sometimes used, including anise, fennel, and caraway. Once the vapor absorbs whatever flavoring is used, it is condensed and diluted (watered down) to make it drinkable.

An early drawing of the tobacco plant and a Native American smoking its leaves. The use of tobacco was firmly established among North American Indians by the time Columbus arrived.

CHAPTER 5

NICOTINE

Nicotine is the principal alkaloid of tobacco, a plant of the genus *Nicotania*. Although there are more than 60 species belonging to this genus, *N. tabacum* is the only one grown commercially. Like the coca plant and the opium poppy, tobacco has become a major cash crop in many countries, including the United States. Moreover, like the coca plant and the opium poppy, nicotine is highly addictive. Heavy smokers who attempt to quit the habit will often suffer unpleasant withdrawal symptoms that are both psychological, such as intense cravings and moodiness, and physiological, such as decreased heart rate, lowered blood pressure, sleep disturbances, and gastrointestinal distress.

Since 1933, the U.S. government has subsidized tobacco growers through a price-support system. Quotas are assigned, restricting the amount of tobacco each grower can cultivate. In return, growers are guaranteed a specific price for their crop. If the market price falls below this price, the government pays the farmer the difference. This subsidization of the tobacco industry, administered by the U.S. Department of Agriculture, is still in effect despite ever-increasing evidence concerning the harmful effects of tobacco's active and addictive ingredient, nicotine.

Sir Walter Raleigh smoking a pipe. Although tobacco use probably dates back to 100 C.E., Raleigh first introduced it to England in 1585, along with the custom of smoking it in a pipe.

The Origins of Tobacco Use

Tobacco smoking probably originated among the Indians of the Western Hemisphere, possibly as early as 100 C.E. Soon after Columbus discovered America, explorers and colonists in North, South, and Central America began to use the leaves of the tobacco plant for smoking, chewing, and snuff-taking. Tobacco was brought to Spain and Portugal by Spanish sailors around 1550, and Sir Walter Raleigh introduced it to England in 1585, along with the custom of smoking it in a pipe.

Soon after the founding of the Jamestown Colony in Virginia in 1607, a man named John Rolfe began cultivating tobacco there. By 1620, Jamestown planters were growing and exporting 100,000 pounds a year. This figure grew to 100 million pounds by the time of the American Revolution.

During the 17th century, tobacco cultivation was the most important industry of the Virginia and Maryland colonies, and somewhat later, of North Carolina. Following the American Revolution, two states west of the Appalachians — Kentucky and Tennessee — became major tobacco growing areas as well. Because the process of growing tobacco required large tracts of land for its cultivation and processing as well as extensive labor forces, it fostered the rise of the plantation system and the introduction of slavery in these colonies.

Many colonial American inns had clay pipes hanging above their hearths. These were for common use; travelers would break off a bit of the stem after smoking. In colonial towns and cities, snuff-taking was considered a more aristocratic use of tobacco. For this purpose, tobacco had to be ground into a fine powder so that it could be inhaled.

Cigar smoking became the most popular way of ingesting tobacco in the late 18th century, especially in Spain and the rest of Europe. Then, as now, cigars were made from small, compact rolls of tobacco leaves. But cigars became less popular 100 years later, replaced by a still more fashionable smoking tool — the cigarette, which is made from more finely cut tobacco than that in cigars, rolled in thin paper.

The event that made the modern cigarette industry possible was the development in the 1880s of the cigarette-making machine. Up until that time, cigarettes were rolled by hand, as were cigars. This was a slow, cumbersome process that did not lend itself to mass production. But now, cigarettes could be produced in the millions.

The first of the tobacco manufacturers to mass-produce cigarettes was Washington, Duke and Sons of Durham, North Carolina. This company soon became the dominant force in the tobacco industry as the American Tobacco Company. In 1911 it was prosecuted under the terms of the Sherman Anti-Trust Act, a law that prevented a specific company from monopolizing an industry, and was broken up into four major companies.

Chewing tobacco, which is the way many Americans enjoyed their tobacco, was so popular during the early 20th century that until the post–World War II era, cuspidors (spittoons) were found in U.S. post offices and in most public buildings. This type of tobacco takes several forms. Some chew plug tobacco, a dense, tightly wrapped wad of tobacco from which a piece is cut for chewing. Another form of chewing tobacco — used mostly in the 1930s and 1940s — was scrap, loose pieces of packaged tobacco.

Types of Tobacco

The tobacco grown in the colonial period in Virginia and Maryland was used for snuff and pipe-smoking. Called Virginia Leaf, it was a dark, air-cured tobacco. (Curing is the process of drying out and preserving tobacco leaves.) Burley tobacco was the result of an accidental mutation of Virginia Leaf that occurred around 1860. Burley had a thinner leaf with a higher degree of absorbency than the dark tobacco popular at that time. Thus, burley could retain flavor well.

Cigarettes roll off the assembly line in a Durham, North Carolina, tobacco plant. Some 56 million Americans smoke, making the manufacture and sale of cigarettes a multibillion dollar industry.

A worker cuts burley tobacco on the Orval Hunt farm near Glasgow, Kentucky. Burley tobacco was discovered as the result of a mutation of Virginia Leaf tobacco and is still used in American cigarettes today.

Gradually, tobacco growing in Virginia moved from the state's fertile tidewater area to its inland Piedmont area, where the soils were thinner and less fertile. Cultivation also spread to the coastal plain of North Carolina, where the soil is similar to that in Virginia's Piedmont area. The change in soil resulted in the emergence of yet another type of tobacco, which, when it was cured, had a lighter, more yellowish color than the older, darker variety. This new strain came to be known as "bright leaf," or simply "bright," tobacco.

The two tobaccos that are used in most American-made cigarettes today are flue-cured and burley tobacco. Smaller amounts of Maryland tobacco are used to make the cigarette burn better, and Turkish tobacco, stronger and more pungent than its American counterpart, is added for flavor.

Growing, Harvesting, and Curing Tobacco

The first phase of tobacco growing is the development of seedlings in a nursery bed or in a hothouse and covered with cheesecloth, plastic, or glass. The seedlings are transplanted when they reach a height of five to six inches. When the seedlings sprout and flower clusters appear, the tops of the plants are removed. This improves the size and quality of the leaves.

About four to six months after planting, the tobacco plant is ready for harvesting, which is done one of two ways. Tobaccos that are to be flue-cured or used for cigar wrappers have their leaves removed from the plants as they ripen. This is called priming. The leaves collected from these plants are hung on sticks. All other tobaccos are stalk-cut and hung on sticks to cure in tobacco barns.

There are three major methods of curing tobacco: air-curing, fire-curing, and flue-curing. Tobacco that is air-cured is placed either directly in the sun or in ventilated tobacco barns. Tobacco that is fire-cured is exposed to the smoke and heat of an open fire burning on the floor of an airtight barn. The process of flue-curing tobacco, the method most commonly used in the United States, involves hanging the tobacco leaves in an airtight barn and then heating them not directly but through a flue.

The Tobacco Industry Around the World

The United States and China are the most important tobacco-growing countries, but the plant is a major crop in other nations throughout the world. The types of tobacco — and methods of curing — vary from country to country. Most tobacco-growing countries in Africa and Central America, for example, favor the flue-curing process, but their tobaccos are darker, and not generally considered equal in quality to the flue-cured tobaccos produced in the United States. Cultivation of the lighter burley tobacco, however, has spread to some Latin American countries and somewhat displaced the production of dark tobaccos indigenous to the area.

The Balkan countries, particularly Greece, Turkey, Yugoslavia, and Bulgaria, produce cigarettes containing a blend of oriental tobaccos. An important component of these cigarettes is latakia, an oriental tobacco with a unique flavor produced by fumigating the tobacco with the smoke of burning pine and oak.

Much of the tobacco grown in India is dark and harsh, and is usually fire-cured. This tobacco is generally smoked in cigars, cheroots (cigars having open, untapered ends), hookahs (pipes that draw the smoke through water), and bidis (inexpensive cigarettes produced from cut tobacco rolled in leaf.)

Some cigar tobacco is cultivated in the United States, but the bulk of it is grown in tropical areas near the equator. An area along the coast of Sumatra is known for the tobacco leaf it produces for cigar wrappers. The finest cigar filler leaves comes from Java and Cuba.

Hazardous to Your Health

The connections between smoking and various diseases has been studied for at least two centuries. In 1775, a paper appeared in a medical journal describing a case of what modern medicine would recognize as mouth cancer. The author

A billboard in Brazil advertises Hollywood-brand cigarettes. All over the world, the tobacco industry attempts to link smoking with robust health and outdoor fun. Mounting scientific evidence gives the lie to this association.

Fewer men are smoking today than in the past. Women, however, continue to smoke as much, if not more, than ever, despite new findings suggesting that smoking complicates pregnancy.

of the paper attributed the disease to pipe smoking. A similar connection between cigar smoking and mouth cancer was reported by a surgeon at Harvard Medical School in the 1830s.

The link between lung cancer and smoking was first demonstrated by a group of doctors in Germany in the late 1930s. Other studies undertaken in the United States and Great Britain corroborated their findings. Since that time, incontrovertible evidence linking smoking to lung cancer and a variety of other diseases — including emphysema, chronic bronchitis, and heart disease—has continued to mount.

Government Actions to Curb Smoking

The first step taken by the federal government to curb smoking occurred in 1964, when the Federal Trade Commission required that all cigarette packages and advertisements bear a health warning stating that smoking could be hazardous to health. The requirements for this cautionary announcement became more specific as evidence regarding the dangers of cigarettes accumulated, and one of the warnings now reads as follows:

> SURGEON GENERAL'S WARNING: Smoking causes lung cancer, heart disease, emphysema, and may complicate pregnancy.

Today, the drive against smoking has become more intense because of findings that constant exposure to the cigarette smoke of others can be injurious to a nonsmoker. For example, there are groups lobbying to have cigarette advertising, which in 1970 was banned from radio and television, outlawed altogether.

Sadly, some 56 million Americans still smoke cigarettes. There is, however, evidence that these numbers may decline as more becomes known about the links between smoking and various diseases. Certainly it is hoped that widespread efforts to educate the public about the considerable dangers of smoking will motivate chronic smokers to kick the habit.

Woman with Coffee *by the French painter Paul Cézanne. The active ingredient in both coffee and tea is caffeine, a powerful nervous system stimulant that provides a morning pick-me-up for millions of people.*

CHAPTER 6

CAFFEINE

Caffeine, which in its pure, unadulterated form is an odorless white powder, is a powerful nervous system stimulant that is the active ingredient in coffee and tea. It is, in fact, the "pick-me-up" effect of caffeine that has made both beverages extremely popular throughout the world.

Drunk in moderation, coffee and tea reduce drowsiness and fatigue, improve mental alertness, and provide quick energy. If ingested in high doses, however, the caffeine in these drinks can cause anxiety symptoms such as nervousness, insomnia, lethargy, irritability, intense headaches, dizziness, tremors, elevated blood pressure, breathlessness, and gastrointestinal disorders. In especially high doses, caffeine can cause irregular heartbeat. The drug is also addictive; people who regularly take caffeine and then try to give it up often experience headaches, fatigue, and muscle pains.

History of Coffee

The coffee plant, or *Coffea arabica*, was first discovered growing wild in Ethiopia as early as 850 C.E. Its cultivation and use soon spread throughout the Islamic world, where coffee was taken up enthusiastically as a substitute for wine, which was forbidden by the Muslim religion.

These early drinkers probably crushed the coffee beans and drank the beverage cold, as a sort of wine. During the 1100s, however, Arabian people began to use the beans to make a hot drink. In the 17th century, European travelers returning from the Near East reported a strange black drink with a delicious flavor, and in 1615, Venetian merchants brought coffee beans back to Europe. The following year, a Dutch trader smuggled a coffee plant to Holland, and by the end of the 17th century the Dutch had established coffee plantations on the Indonesian island of Java.

It was around this time that the first coffee houses opened, in Vienna. Turks who had invaded the city left behind sacks of coffee beans upon retreating. An enterprising Vien-

A Persian miniature depicting a group of men drinking coffee. Coffee is extremely popular throughout the Islamic world as a substitute for wine, which is forbidden by the Muslim religion.

nese discovered them, learned how to roast the beans and prepare them for drinking, and opened a coffee house. This was the beginning of a proliferation of coffee houses throughout Europe and the beginning of a "coffee craze" that inspired Johann Sebastian Bach to compose his "Coffee Cantata" in praise of the beverage.

Coffee drinking attained even greater popularity when the custom crossed the Atlantic and took root in North America. Today, most Americans would not think of starting the day or getting through a daily work routine without their daily ration of coffee.

Instant Coffee

Instant coffee is produced by removing the water — either by evaporating or freezing — from a concentrated extract of ground roast coffee. Although it was first marketed as long ago as the second decade of the 20th century, the armed forces' demand for instant coffee in World War II accelerated its use. By 1953, 1 cup of coffee in 10 drunk by Americans was instant coffee. Wartime technology also led to freeze-dried coffee, as the use of this technique for army rations was later applied to coffee.

History of Tea

The custom of drinking tea originated in China as far back as 2500 B.C.E. According to legend, the beverage was discovered by a Chinese philosopher who smelled a delicious aroma after tea leaves had accidentally spilled into his water. Tea drinking spread to Japan in the Middle Ages and in the 17th century to continental Europe and Great Britain, where it became the beverage of choice.

During this time tea also became popular in the North American colonies, whose refusal to pay British-imposed tariffs on tea culminated in a revolt in 1773. Colonists dressed as Indians dumped hundreds of chests of tea owned by an important British trading company into the Boston harbor. This incident, known as the Boston Tea Party, was one of the immediate triggers of the American Revolution.

During the 17th and 18th centuries, the British had a near monopoly on the tea trade, based on a commercial treaty with China, the source at the time of most teas. When the

A 19th-century painting of Chinese tea cultivation. The custom of tea drinking originated in China more than 4,000 years ago.

treaty expired in 1833, however, British control of the tea trade became increasingly insecure. This new vulnerability was not helped by a domestic tax on tea that was at the time 15 times higher than the tax on coffee. This turn of events caused coffee to become more popular in Britain than tea. This trend lasted until the mid-19th century, when tea taxes were lowered and tea once again became the British beverage of choice, a status it continues to enjoy to this day.

Cultivating Coffee

There are three species of coffee. *Coffea arabica*, native to Ethiopia, is now cultivated chiefly in Brazil and Colombia; *Coffea robusta*, native to Saudi Arabia, is now cultivated chiefly in Indonesia, Brazil, and many parts of Africa; and *Coffea liberica*, native to Liberia, is currently cultivated in Africa. Until about a century ago, arabica was the only species cultivated. It has a superior flavor to all other species of coffee and is in fact used to make about 75% of the coffee in the world. But because it is especially vulnerable to attacks by disease and insects, the more resistant robusta species was developed. Robusta has more than double the caffeine content of arabica, and, consequently, a greater stimulating action. Because of this high caffeine content and a higher content of soluble extracts, robusta is preferred for use in the manufacture of instant coffee.

Coffee grows best in tropical climates at altitudes of 2,000 to 6,000 feet above sea level. The ideal soil for coffee growing has a high potash (a potassium compound) content and good drainage. The slopes of an extinct volcano provide an ideal site for coffee cultivation.

The coffee "tree," which is actually an evergreen shrub, generally starts from seeds planted on hillsides or in seedbeds (from which the young plants are later transplanted to a hilly site). As the trees grow, they are generally pruned to a height of 6 feet to make harvesting easier (undomesticated coffee trees grow to a height of 14 to 30 feet). The leaves of the trees are dark green, glossy on top and a lighter, duller green on the underside. During the growing season, the trees are sprayed with insecticides and fungicides to ward off disease and attacks by insects.

Following the blooming and wilting of small white blossoms on the tree, small berries appear that change from green to deep red as they ripen. The ripening process takes about six months. An examination of the berry at this time would reveal a fleshy pulp beneath its skin and within the pulp a parchmentlike covering that encloses the green beans. There are usually two beans to each berry.

Coffee growing is a long-term venture; it normally takes five years before a coffee tree bears fruit, and eight years before it yields a coffee bean of satisfactory, commercial quality. Most coffee trees bear fruit for 15 to 20 years; some may yield for a longer period where soil conditions are favorable.

Harvesting and Processing Coffee

Harvesting coffee berries is an intensive process that often involves many people. The berries are picked by hand and are then soaked in water overnight to loosen and remove the skins and pulp surrounding the beans, which then undergo a fermentation process to remove their gummy coating. Following fermentation, the beans are washed and dried. In areas where water is scarce, a drying process is used to separate the beans from their outer layers.

The coffee beans are usually not roasted until they reach the country in which they will be consumed. The roasting takes place in revolving, perforated metal cylinders, at a temperature of about 400 to 500° Fahrenheit. The process takes from 5 to 15 minutes, depending upon the degree of roasting desired. The longer coffee is roasted, the darker is its color and the more concentrated its caffeine content. There are different national preferences: Americans, for example, prefer a medium roast; French and Italian coffee drinkers prefer a darker roast; and Turks like their coffee pitch black.

Following roasting, the coffee is cooled before grinding. After grinding, which breaks the beans into small particles,

Pickers on a Colombian plantation empty baskets of coffee berries into a waiting truck. Coffea arabica, the type of coffee cultivated in Colombia, is used to make about 75% of the coffee in the world.

Workers ready coffee for shipment in Ecuador. After the coffee is shipped to the country in which it will be consumed, it is roasted and then cooled before grinding.

the coffee is packaged in vacuum cans or paper bags, and the finished product is ready for shipment. Of course, people who wish to buy their coffee in bean form and grind it themselves just before brewing it can do so.

Cultivating and Harvesting Tea

The tea plant, *Camellia sinensis*, has a great number of varieties, or subspecies. Considerable confusion once existed as to whether there was one or more species of the plant, but in 1958 it was internationally agreed that there is one species with several varieties, two of which have major commercial importance.

Like the coffee plant, the tea plant is an evergreen tree or bush that grows in the tropics or subtropics. It grows best at altitudes of 2,000 to 6,500 feet and in areas that receive moderate rainfall. The most cultivated variety is Assam tea, or *assamica*, which because of its low resistance to cold survives best in tropical areas. China tea, or *sinensis*, has lower yields than Assam tea but produces a more delicately flavored beverage. It can tolerate brief cold periods and thus higher altitudes than Assam tea. In the late 1800s, China tea

An Indian woman plucks the leaves from a tea plant. After the tea leaves are picked they are either dried in the sun and squeezed for black tea or steamed dry for green tea.

was cultivated in South Carolina, but the plantations were abandoned because high labor costs made them unprofitable. However, many wild tea plants still survive in this area.

Tea plants usually live 25 to 50 years, and the leaves are usually first ready for plucking when the plant is in its fifth year. After the leaves are picked they are treated in one of two ways. Leaves that are harvested for black tea, which is used to make about three-fourths of all teas, are dried in the sun and then squeezed to release their sap. Leaves for green tea, which is the tea served in many Chinese restaurants, are steamed dry; this process usually results in a more bitter tea. Both teas contain about the same amount of caffeine. After manufacturing the tea is packed in foil-lined cases and shipped to blenders, who then package the tea, either loose or in bags.

The World Coffee Economy

Brazil is the world's leading producer and exporter of coffee. In order of importance, the other major coffee-exporting countries in the Western Hemisphere are Colombia, El Salvador, Guatemala, Mexico, Costa Rica, Ecuador, Peru, Nicaragua, Honduras, Haiti, the Dominican Republic, and Venezuela. The importance of coffee to the economy of these Latin American countries is indicated by the fact that coffee represents one-fifth of their exports. In Asia and Africa, the principal coffee-exporting countries are the Ivory Coast, Angola, Ethiopia, Indonesia, Cameroon, Madagascar, Kenya, Zaire, Tanzania, India, and Burundi.

Although Americans are known as heavy coffee drinkers, the United States ranks seventh among coffee-consuming nations. The first six are Denmark, Finland, Norway, Switzerland, Belgium, and the Netherlands.

Because the worldwide coffee crop is sensitive to the vagaries of weather and natural disasters such as flood, fire, and disease, the amount of coffee available to the world market can vary considerably from year to year. In good years, this has led to serious crop gluts; one in Brazil in the 1930s, for instance, forced that nation to burn a large portion of the crop.

Since that time, several international organizations have attempted to stabilize the world coffee trade by imposing coffee export quotas, thereby controlling production. The current organization, known as the International Coffee Organization, established in 1983, attempts to control the flow of coffee coming on the international market but does not fix prices.

Tea Trading and Consumption

The leading exporter of tea in the world is India, followed, in order, by China, Sri Lanka, the Soviet Union, Japan, Kenya, and Turkey. The major importers of tea are Great Britain, the United States, and Pakistan.

Although trade in tea has not been strictly regulated since the 1930s, the governments of the individual exporting nations have controlled it since that time. Opponents of regulation have argued that official control is unnecessary because the price of tea has been fairly stable. In recent years, however, tea prices have risen sharply, and there are currently discussions about the possibility of starting an International Tea Agreement, which would be similar in structure and purpose to the International Coffee Organization.

Other Sources of Caffeine

Cola drinks, which are extracted from the nuts of the tree *Cola nitrida*, also contain caffeine. The amount tends to vary

A worker controls the flow of coffee through pipelines and into huge vats at an instant-coffee plant in New Orleans. The coffee is turned into a concentrated liquid and then into powder.

from brand to brand, but a bottle of cola has an average of about one-third to one-half the amount of caffeine in the same amount of coffee. Another source of caffeine is cocoa, although the amount is relatively small in comparison with that in coffee or tea. The stimulating effect of cocoa is mainly the result of the presence of another chemical, theobromine.

The Switch to Decaffeinated Beverages

Because the side effects resulting from heavy, habitual use of coffee and other caffeinated beverages have been so widely publicized in recent years, and interest in dietary health has increased, there has been an accelerated trend toward consumption of decaffeinated colas, and, especially, decaffeinated coffee.

A few years ago, questions were raised about the safety of decaffeinated beverages themselves. The concern had to do with the chemicals used in the decaffeination process patented by a German chemist in 1908. His method employed a solvent to draw 97 to 98% of the caffeine out of the beans. The solvent commonly used, trichloroethylene, was found to cause liver cancer in mice.

Many manufacturers then switched to other solvents, such as methylene chloride, that had not been linked to cancer. Other coffee producers began using natural solvents such as ethyl acetate, a chemical found in bananas and pineapples. Another decaffeination process, used by coffee producers in Switzerland and Belgium, uses water instead of a chemical as the solvent.

Close to one-third of all coffee drinkers now drink the decaffeinated variety. Brands of decaffeinated coffee, some on the market for only a few years, have become top sellers. And for those who prefer to brew their own coffee, decaffeinated beans are now available.

A Haitian artist's blend of reality and fantasy takes the form of a humanoid plant. The effects of natural plant substances are often extremely powerful and can include severe distortions of reality.

CHAPTER 7

HALLUCINOGENIC DRUGS FROM PLANTS

The term hallucination comes from the Latin verb *halluci-nari*, "to wander in the mind"; a hallucinogen is in fact a drug that creates such an effect. There are different types of hallucinogens. Marijuana and hashish, for example, are relatively mild hallucinogens. The distortions of reality these hemp products produce are usually not extremely powerful. The strongest hallucinogens are those that are synthetically created through chemical processes, such as LSD. This chapter, however, is concerned only with hallucinogens, other than hemp products, that are derived from natural plant substances.

Peyote

Peyote is the name for the cactus genus *Lophophora*, native to the desert regions of central and northern Mexico. The hallucinogenic drug comes from the plant's top crown, the center of which contains a mass of white hair in which small flowers are concealed. When the tops are sliced off the cactus and allowed to dry, they become hard and brittle and shrink to button-shaped disks, an inch or two in diameter and less than half an inch in thickness.

A Zapotecan deity is depicted on an 8th-century C.E. funerary urn. There is evidence that the Zapotecs, an advanced civilization that flourished in Mexico before the arrival of the Europeans, used naturally derived psychoactive substances during religious ceremonies.

These disks, which are called mescal buttons, are sucked and then swallowed whole. The buttons have a bitter taste similar to that of orange rind and an unpleasant odor. It usually takes several buttons to achieve a hallucinatory effect. Persons ingesting mescal buttons usually become nauseated.

Peyote intoxication usually induces brightly colored visions, sometimes of totally imaginary figures and shapes. Sense perceptions, particularly hearing, seem intensified. The hallucinator often experiences heightened mental awareness and sometimes feels anxiety or even terror. Common physiological effects of this drug include dilation of the eyes, chills, and vomiting.

Use of Peyote Among the Indians

It is believed that peyote was used for hallucinogenic purposes by natives of what is now the southwestern United States and northern Mexico for more than 2,000 years. Spanish explorers in the 16th century noted the use of peyote by Aztec priests in their healing and religious rites.

Around the turn of the 20th century, the ceremonial use of the drug spread northward to more than 30 Indian tribes throughout the United States. At various times since then, there have been attempts by the government, missionaries, and Indians opposed to the practice to suppress the use of peyote and stop the fast-growing peyote cult. Several western states passed laws banning its use, and the federal government made an active effort to suppress the trafficking of the drug during Prohibition (1919–33). The state laws concerning peyote have since been repealed, and the federal government permits its use within the context of a specific religious organization called the Native American church, which is composed of peyote-using tribal groups.

Services of the Native American church take place around an altar fire where the communicants take peyote and experience their visions to the beat of a drum. This service usually lasts all night; the nausea and vomiting experienced

An American Indian woman cuts a stalk off of a peyote cactus. Peyote is still used in the religious ceremonies of the Native American church.

A stone carving from Guatemala shows an animal with a mushroom growing from its back. Figures such as this have been associated with traditional native mushroom cults dating back more than 2,000 years.

by many of the participants is considered part of a purging or cleansing process. The Native American church claims a membership of 200,000, drawn from tribes throughout the United States and Canada.

Except for its use within the Native American church, peyote is prohibited by federal law. In addition, there is no significant traffic in the drug and little interest in it among drug abusers because of the nausea and vomiting associated with its use.

Mescaline

Although the Indians of Mexico had been aware of the hallucinogenic properties of the peyote cactus for centuries, it was not until 1897 that mescaline, the principal hallucinogenic alkaloid in the plant, was identified and isolated. On November 23 of that year, Arthur Heffter, a German professsor of pharmacology, ingested 150 milligrams of mescaline and reported the following vision:

Violet and green spots appear on the paper during readings. When the eyes are kept shut the following visual images occur . . . carpet patterns, ribbed vaulting, etc. . . . later on, landscapes, halls, architectural scenes also appear.

In 1918, the chemical structure of mescaline was determined, making possible its synthesis in a laboratory. Mescaline, or 3,4,5-trimethoxyphenylethylamine, is one of a large group of psychedelic compounds with simple one-ring chemical structures. Mescaline is the only one found in nature. The laboratory synthesis of mescaline made it a more desirable drug than peyote, mescaline in its natural state, because the synthetic drug induced a hallucinogenic state more rapidly and did not cause nausea and vomiting.

As a result, there was considerable intellectual interest in the drug in the early part of the century. Two eminent English men of letters, Havelock Ellis, the psychologist, and Aldous Huxley, the novelist and essayist, both experimented with mescaline and then wrote of their experiences with the drug.

Mescaline is not an important street drug, and there is no substantial trafficking network. Under the Controlled Substances Act, mescaline is identified — along with heroin and LSD—as a hallucinogen.

The Sacred Mushrooms

Psychoactive mushrooms, called *teonanactyl*, or "flesh of the gods," by the Aztecs, were actually used well before this ancient Indian tribe discovered their mind-altering properties in 1300 C.E. In fact, ancient statues of giant mushrooms found in El Salvador and Guatemala suggest that these organic hallucinogens were used in these regions as early as 1000 B.C.E. Other evidence indicates that the Maya, Toltec, and Nahua Indian civilizations, all predecessors of the Aztecs, partook of the so-called sacred mushrooms.

The Aztecs, however, tried to restrict the use of the mushrooms to religious ceremonies and to royal banquets where war prisoners were sacrificed to appease the sun god. One of these celebrated feasts was the coronation of Montezuma II in 1502. The war prisoners were slain and their hearts were offered in sacrifice to the gods. After partaking of the flesh of these victims, the guests took teonanactyl and "spoke to the gods."

Although the use of the sacred mushrooms by the Mexican Indians in religious rites and ceremonies continued through the centuries and persists today, little was known about it outside of that culture until 1936. That year, an anthropologist discovered the use of the mushrooms in ceremonies of the Mazatec tribe and took a mushroom specimen that was eventually identified as a lineal descendent of teonanactyl eaten by the Aztecs. In 1953, R. Gordon Wasson and Roger Heim identified several more species of mushrooms with hallucinogenic properties, and it is believed there are still other species not yet classified.

In 1958, Dr. Albert Hofmann, who 15 years earlier had synthesized LSD, isolated *psilocybin*, which is the hallucinogenic alkaloid in the mushrooms. He was later able to synthesize psilocybin, which is chemically related to *lysergic acid diethylamide* (LSD) and produces similar visions and hallucinations.

A Chinese painting of morning glory flowers. The seeds of certain members of the morning glory family contain natural hallucinogens that are very similar in chemical structure to the synthetic hallucinogen LSD.

The ingestion of psychoactive mushrooms is still an active part of religious rituals among some Mexican Indian tribes. Twelve of these bitter-tasting, acrid-smelling mushrooms are usually enough to evoke hallucinatory visions. The physical reactions, which come before the hallucinations, include nausea, muscle relaxation, and dilation of the pupils. Then comes an abrupt mood change — some users experience wild hilarity — and hallucinations. The visions often consist of brilliantly colored shapes and geometric patterns and frequently last four to five hours. This period of intense hallucination is usually followed by a feeling of mental and physical depression and an inability to perceive time and space. Excessively large doses of the mushrooms can be fatal.

Although there was some minor illicit traffic in psychedelic mushrooms in the United States during the 1960s and 1970s — when the interest in psychedelic drugs was widespread — the mushroom is no longer a significant street drug. The active component, psilocybin, which is expensive to synthesize, is classified as a Schedule I drug under the Controlled Substance Act.

Morning Glory Seeds

LSD is a synthetic, or manmade, drug. But there are also natural sources of lysergic acid. These substances, called ergot alkaloids, can be found in certain members of the *Convolvulaceae*, or morning glory family, notably *Rivea corymbosa* and *Ipomoea violacea*.

Both species are cultivated in several horticultural varieties, all of which contain various forms of lysergic acid, which is only 5 to 10% as potent as LSD. In order to achieve the hallucinatory effects comparable to those produced by 200 to 300 micrograms of LSD — an experience that could last 4 to 14 hours — one must ingest 100 to 300 seeds. Morning-glory seeds can be ground and brewed as a tea, but they are generally ingested by being chewed or swallowed whole.

The morning-glory species *Rivea corymbosa* is what the Aztecs called *oloiuqui* and used in their religious rituals. This and other species of morning glories have been used by Mexican Indians for centuries. The hallucinations caused by the seeds are used by these tribes to foretell future events and to diagnose and treat various illnesses.

American drug users became interested in morning-glory seeds in the 1960s, when scientific journals published articles relating them to LSD. However, use of the seeds as a recreational drug has been discouraged by commercial seed producers, who treat the seeds with a poisonous coating that cannot be removed by washing and can cause unpleasant side effects such as nausea, vomiting, and severe abdominal pain. Extremely high doses of the seeds can cause psychotic reactions, heart failure, and shock.

Nutmeg

Nutmeg is a spice consisting of the seed of the *Myristica fragrans*, a tropical evergreen tree grown in the Moluccas and the East Indies. It was brought to Europe in the 17th century by Dutch explorers. Because of its distinctive pungent fragrance and sweet taste, nutmeg is used as a flavoring for baked goods, candies, puddings, meats, and beverages such as eggnog.

The trees bearing the nutmeg grow to a height of about 65 feet and yield the nutmeg fruit 8 years after planting. The fruit of the tree is similar in appearance to an apricot. It splits in two when it is fully ripened, revealing a crimson-covered mace or hull covering the nutmeg seed. The maces are dried in the sun for a period of six to eight weeks. Then the nutmeg seeds are removed for further processing.

The effects of a 10-gram dose of nutmeg, which is almost always eaten, is equivalent to one marijuana cigarette, but the sensation is often accompanied by severe diarrhea and nausea. When more than 10 grams are taken, the effects of the drug may become more intense but the side effects also tend to be more severe — dizziness, flushes, dry mouth and throat, accelerated heartbeat, constipation, urinary difficulty, and occasionally, panic. Nutmeg seldom causes powerful hallucinations, simply because the dosage required to reach that state is dangerously close to a toxic overdose.

Because of the unpleasant consequences of its use, nutmeg is not a popular street drug. Its chief abusers tend to be people such as prisoners who do not have access to other drugs. And because of its legal status, an illicit underground trafficking network for this substance does not exist.

Conclusion

Through the ages, human beings have cultivated a number of plants for their mood- and mind-altering powers. Such natural substances are found all over the world and are used in religious ceremonies, as economic commodities, for their medicinal properties, and for recreational purposes. Human beings have shown an extraordinary amount of ingenuity in first discovering and then refining these grains, berries, mushrooms, cacti, and leaves into edible and drinkable products. It is unfortunate that the same amount of know-how is not always brought to bear in deciding how, when, and in what quantities these psychoactive drugs will be consumed.

APPENDIX

State Agencies
for the Prevention and Treatment
of Drug Abuse

ALABAMA
Department of Mental Health
Division of Mental Illness and
   Substance Abuse Community
   Programs
200 Interstate Park Drive
P.O. Box 3710
Montgomery, AL 36193
(205) 271-9253

ALASKA
Department of Health and Social
   Services
Office of Alcoholism and Drug
   Abuse
Pouch H-05-F
Juneau, AK 99811
(907) 586-6201

ARIZONA
Department of Health Services
Division of Behavioral Health
   Services
Bureau of Community Services
Alcohol Abuse and Alcoholism
   Section
2500 East Van Buren
Phoenix, AZ 85008
(602) 255-1238

Department of Health Services
Division of Behavioral Health
   Services
Bureau of Community Services
Drug Abuse Section
2500 East Van Buren
Phoenix, AZ 85008
(602) 255-1240

ARKANSAS
Department of Human Services
Office of Alcohol and Drug Abuse
   Prevention
1515 West 7th Avenue
Suite 310
Little Rock, AR 72202
(501) 371-2603

CALIFORNIA
Department of Alcohol and Drug
   Abuse
111 Capitol Mall
Sacramento, CA 95814
(916) 445-1940

COLORADO
Department of Health
Alcohol and Drug Abuse Division
4210 East 11th Avenue
Denver, CO 80220
(303) 320-6137

CONNECTICUT
Alcohol and Drug Abuse
   Commission
999 Asylum Avenue
3rd Floor
Hartford, CT 06105
(203) 566-4145

DELAWARE
Division of Mental Health
Bureau of Alcoholism and Drug
   Abuse
1901 North Dupont Highway
Newcastle, DE 19720
(302) 421-6101

DISTRICT OF COLUMBIA
Department of Human Services
Office of Health Planning and
 Development
601 Indiana Avenue, NW
Suite 500
Washington, D.C. 20004
(202) 724-5641

FLORIDA
Department of Health and
 Rehabilitative Services
Alcoholic Rehabilitation Program
1317 Winewood Boulevard
Room 187A
Tallahassee, FL 32301
(904) 488-0396

Department of Health and
 Rehabilitative Services
Drug Abuse Program
1317 Winewood Boulevard
Building 6, Room 155
Tallahassee, FL 32301
(904) 488-0900

GEORGIA
Department of Human Resources
Division of Mental Health and
 Mental Retardation
Alcohol and Drug Section
618 Ponce De Leon Avenue, NE
Atlanta, GA 30365-2101
(404) 894-4785

HAWAII
Department of Health
Mental Health Division
Alcohol and Drug Abuse Branch
1250 Punch Bowl Street
P.O. Box 3378
Honolulu, HI 96801
(808) 548-4280

IDAHO
Department of Health and Welfare
Bureau of Preventive Medicine
Substance Abuse Section
450 West State
Boise, ID 83720
(208) 334-4368

ILLINOIS
Department of Mental Health and
 Developmental Disabilities
Division of Alcoholism
160 North La Salle Street
Room 1500
Chicago, IL 60601
(312) 793-2907

Illinois Dangerous Drugs
 Commission
300 North State Street
Suite 1500
Chicago, IL 60610
(312) 822-9860

INDIANA
Department of Mental Health
Division of Addiction Services
429 North Pennsylvania Street
Indianapolis, IN 46204
(317) 232-7816

IOWA
Department of Substance Abuse
505 5th Avenue
Insurance Exchange Building
Suite 202
Des Moines, IA 50319
(515) 281-3641

KANSAS
Department of Social Rehabilitation
Alcohol and Drug Abuse Services
2700 West 6th Street
Biddle Building
Topeka, KS 66606
(913) 296-3925

KENTUCKY
Cabinet for Human Resources
Department of Health Services
Substance Abuse Branch
275 East Main Street
Frankfort, KY 40601
(502) 564-2880

LOUISIANA
Department of Health and Human
  Resources
Office of Mental Health and
  Substance Abuse
655 North 5th Street
P.O. Box 4049
Baton Rouge, LA 70821
(504) 342-2565

MAINE
Department of Human Services
Office of Alcoholism and Drug
  Abuse Prevention
Bureau of Rehabilitation
32 Winthrop Street
Augusta, ME 04330
(207) 289-2781

MARYLAND
Alcoholism Control Administration
201 West Preston Street
Fourth Floor
Baltimore, MD 21201
(301) 383-2977

State Health Department
Drug Abuse Administration
201 West Preston Street
Baltimore, MD 21201
(301) 383-3312

MASSACHUSETTS
Department of Public Health
Division of Alcoholism
755 Boylston Street
Sixth Floor
Boston, MA 02116
(617) 727-1960

Department of Public Health
Division of Drug Rehabilitation
600 Washington Street
Boston, MA 02114
(617) 727-8617

MICHIGAN
Department of Public Health
Office of Substance Abuse Services
3500 North Logan Street
P.O. Box 30035
Lansing, MI 48909
(517) 373-8603

MINNESOTA
Department of Public Welfare
Chemical Dependency Program
  Division
Centennial Building
658 Cedar Street
4th Floor
Saint Paul, MN 55155
(612) 296-4614

MISSISSIPPI
Department of Mental Health
Division of Alcohol and Drug Abuse
1102 Robert E. Lee Building
Jackson, MS 39201
(601) 359-1297

MISSOURI
Department of Mental Health
Division of Alcoholism and Drug
  Abuse
2002 Missouri Boulevard
P.O. Box 687
Jefferson City, MO 65102
(314) 751-4942

MONTANA
Department of Institutions
Alcohol and Drug Abuse Division
1539 11th Avenue
Helena, MT 59620
(406) 449-2827

NEBRASKA
Department of Public Institutions
Division of Alcoholism and Drug
Abuse
801 West Van Dorn Street
P.O. Box 94728
Lincoln, NB 68509
(402) 471-2851, Ext. 415

NEVADA
Department of Human Resources
Bureau of Alcohol and Drug Abuse
505 East King Street
Carson City, NV 89710
(702) 885-4790

NEW HAMPSHIRE
Department of Health and Welfare
Office of Alcohol and Drug Abuse
  Prevention
Hazen Drive
Health and Welfare Building
Concord, NH 03301
(603) 271-4627

NEW JERSEY
Department of Health
Division of Alcoholism
129 East Hanover Street CN 362
Trenton, NJ 08625
(609) 292-8949

Department of Health
Division of Narcotic and Drug
  Abuse Control
129 East Hanover Street CN 362
Trenton, NJ 08625
(609) 292-8949

NEW MEXICO
Health and Environment Department
Behavioral Services Division
Substance Abuse Bureau
725 Saint Michaels Drive
P.O. Box 968
Santa Fe, NM 87503
(505) 984-0020, Ext. 304

NEW YORK
Division of Alcoholism and Alcohol
  Abuse
194 Washington Avenue
Albany, NY 12210
(518) 474-5417

Division of Substance Abuse
  Services
Executive Park South
Box 8200
Albany, NY 12203
(518) 457-7629

NORTH CAROLINA
Department of Human Resources
Division of Mental Health, Mental
  Retardation and Substance Abuse
  Services
Alcohol and Drug Abuse Services
325 North Salisbury Street
Albemarle Building
Raleigh, NC 27611
(919) 733-4670

NORTH DAKOTA
Department of Human Services
Division of Alcoholism and Drug
  Abuse
State Capitol Building
Bismarck, ND 58505
(701) 224-2767

OHIO
Department of Health
Division of Alcoholism
246 North High Street
P.O. Box 118
Columbus, OH 43216
(614) 466-3543

Department of Mental Health
Bureau of Drug Abuse
65 South Front Street
Columbus, OH 43215
(614) 466-9023

OKLAHOMA
Department of Mental Health
Alcohol and Drug Programs
4545 North Lincoln Boulevard
Suite 100 East Terrace
P.O. Box 53277
Oklahoma City, OK 73152
(405) 521-0044

OREGON
Department of Human Resources
Mental Health Division
Office of Programs for Alcohol and
Drug Problems
2575 Bittern Street, NE
Salem, OR 97310
(503) 378-2163

PENNSYLVANIA
Department of Health
Office of Drug and Alcohol
Programs
Commonwealth and Forster Avenues
Health and Welfare Building
P.O. Box 90
Harrisburg, PA 17108
(717) 787-9857

RHODE ISLAND
Department of Mental Health,
Mental Retardation and Hospitals
Division of Substance Abuse
Substance Abuse Administration
Building
Cranston, RI 02920
(401) 464-2091

SOUTH CAROLINA
Commission on Alcohol and Drug
Abuse
3700 Forest Drive
Columbia, SC 29204
(803) 758-2521

SOUTH DAKOTA
Department of Health
Division of Alcohol and Drug Abuse
523 East Capitol, Joe Foss Building
Pierre, SD 57501
(605) 773-4806

TENNESSEE
Department of Mental Health and
Mental Retardation
Alcohol and Drug Abuse Services
505 Deaderick Street
James K. Polk Building,
Fourth Floor
Nashville, TN 37219
(615) 741-1921

TEXAS
Commission on Alcoholism
809 Sam Houston State Office
Building
Austin, TX 78701
(512) 475-2577
Department of Community Affairs
Drug Abuse Prevention Division
2015 South Interstate Highway 35
P.O. Box 13166
Austin, TX 78711
(512) 443-4100

UTAH
Department of Social Services
Division of Alcoholism and Drugs
150 West North Temple
Suite 350
P.O. Box 2500
Salt Lake City, UT 84110
(801) 533-6532

VERMONT
Agency of Human Services
Department of Social and
Rehabilitation Services
Alcohol and Drug Abuse Division
103 South Main Street
Waterbury, VT 05676
(802) 241-2170

VIRGINIA
Department of Mental Health and
  Mental Retardation
Division of Substance Abuse
109 Governor Street
P.O. Box 1797
Richmond, VA 23214
(804) 786-5313

WASHINGTON
Department of Social and Health
  Service
Bureau of Alcohol and Substance
  Abuse
Office Building—44 W
Olympia, WA 98504
(206) 753-5866

WEST VIRGINIA
Department of Health
Office of Behavioral Health Services
Division on Alcoholism and Drug
  Abuse
1800 Washington Street East
Building 3 Room 451
Charleston, WV 25305
(304) 348-2276

WISCONSIN
Department of Health and Social
  Services
Division of Community Services
Bureau of Community Programs
Alcohol and Other Drug Abuse
  Program Office
1 West Wilson Street
P.O. Box 7851
Madison, WI 53707
(608) 266-2717

WYOMING
Alcohol and Drug Abuse Programs
Hathaway Building
Cheyenne, WY 82002
(307) 777-7115, Ext. 7118

GUAM
Mental Health & Substance Abuse
  Agency
P.O. Box 20999
Guam 96921

PUERTO RICO
Department of Addiction Control
  Services
Alcohol Abuse Programs
P.O. Box B-Y Rio Piedras Station
Rio Piedras, PR 00928
(809) 763-5014

Department of Addiction Control
  Services
Drug Abuse Programs
P.O. Box B-Y Rio Piedras Station
Rio Piedras, PR 00928
(809) 764-8140

VIRGIN ISLANDS
Division of Mental Health,
  Alcoholism & Drug Dependency
  Services
P.O. Box 7329
Saint Thomas, Virgin Islands 00801
(809) 774-7265

AMERICAN SAMOA
LBJ Tropical Medical Center
Department of Mental Health Clinic
Pago Pago, American Samoa 96799

TRUST TERRITORIES
Director of Health Services
Office of the High Commissioner
Saipan, Trust Territories 96950

Further Reading

Amerine, Maynard A., and Vernon L. Singleton. *Wine: An Introduction*. Berkeley, CA: University of California Press, 1978.

Grinspoon, Lester, and James B. Bakalar. *Psychedelic Drugs Reconsidered*. New York: Basic Books, 1981.

Haarer, Alec E. *Coffee Growing*. New York: Oxford University Press, 1963.

Johnson, Phillip R. *The Economics of the Tobacco Industry*. New York: Praeger, 1984.

Lawran, B. "Killer Weed." *Omni*, September 1985.

Lingeman, Richard R. *Drugs from A to Z*. New York: McGraw-Hill, 1974.

Office of Public Affairs, Drug Enforcement Administration. *Narcotics Intelligence Estimate*. Washington, D.C.: U.S Government Printing Office, 1984.

U. S. Department of State, Bureau of International Narcotics Matters. *International Narcotics Control Strategy Report*. March 1987.

Young, Lawrence A. *Recreational Drugs*. New York: Collier Books, 1977.

Glossary

addiction a condition caused by repeated drug use, characterized by a compulsive urge to continue using the drug, a tendency to increase the dosage, and physiological and/or psychological dependence

alcohol any of a series of hydroxylcompounds that includes ethanol and methanol; intoxicating liquor containing alcohol

alkaloid any of the nitrogen-containing organic bases obtained from plants, including nicotine, quinine, cocaine, and morphine

bitartrates acidic additives used in some wines

caffeine a white, odorless powder in its pure form; a powerful stimulant to the central nervous system

cocaine the primary psychoactive ingredient in the coca plant; a behavioral stimulant

crack an adulterated, highly addictive form of cocaine

distillation a heat-dependent process used to purify or isolate a fraction of a complex substance, especially the vaporization of a liquid mixture with subsequent cooling to condensation

ergot alkaloids natural sources of lysergic acid

ethanol a colorless, volatile liquid present in distilled liquors and obtained from grain by fermentation

euphoria a mental high characterized by a sense of well-being

fermentation the process by which yeast converts sugar to carbon dioxide and alcohol in the absence of oxygen

hallucinogen a drug that produces sensory impressions that have no basis in reality

hashish an extract prepared from the flowers, stalks, leaves, and resin of the hemp, or marijuana, plant, which is smoked for its euphoric effects

hepatitis inflammation of the liver marked by jaundice and caused by infectious or toxic agents

heroin a semisynthetic opiate produced by a chemical modification of morphine

LSD lysergic acid diethylamide; a hallucinogenic drug derived either from a fungus that grows on rye or from morning-glory seeds

mescaline a psychedelic drug found in the peyote cactus

morphine an opiate used as a sedative and pain reliever

narcotic originally, referring to a group of drugs producing effects similar to those of morphine; often used to refer to any substance that sedates, has a depressive side effect, and/or causes dependence

nicotine a poisonous alkaloid found in tobacco; believed to be responsible for the addictive properties of cigarettes

opiate a compound derived from the milky juice of the poppy plant *Papaver somniferum*, including opium, morphine, codeine, and heroin

quinine a bitter, colorless crystalline powder, obtained from cinchona bark and used as an antimalarial drug

physical dependence an adaptation of the body to the presence of a drug such that its absence produces withdrawal symptoms

psilocybin a strongly hallucinogenic compound derived from the mushroom *Psilocybe mexicana*

psychological dependence a condition in which the drug user craves a drug to maintain a sense of well-being and feels discomfort when deprived of it

septicemia a condition in which disease-causing microorganisms or their toxins are present in the bloodstream

sinsemilla "without seeds"; a variety of the cannabis plant

sulfuric acid a corrosive, dense acidused in the manufacture of a variety of chemicals

THC tetrahydrocannabinol; the psychoactive ingredient in marijuana

tolerance a decrease in susceptibility to the effects of a drug due to its continued administration, resulting in the user's need to increase the drug dosage in order to achieve the effects previously experienced

whiskey a liquor distilled from corn, rye, or barley

withdrawal the psychological and physiological effects of discontinued drug use

PICTURE CREDITS

Fratelli Allinari/Art Resource: p. 12; AP/Wide World Photos: pp. 8, 25, 26, 27, 30, 35, 39, 40, 42, 48, 51, 52, 54, 65, 66, 69, 71, 78, 79, 90, 92, 94; Art Resource: pp. 81, 91; The Bettmann Archive: pp. 61, 74, 76; Bildarchive Foto Marburg/Art Resource: p. 44; Daniel S. Brody/Art Resource: p. 68; Free Library of Philadelphia/Art Resource: p. 102; Giraudon/Art Resource: pp. 18, 22, 34, 56, 59, 84, 86, 98; Alan Keler/Art Resource: p. 64; Lauros-Giraudon/Art Resource: p. 100; Eugene Luttenberg/Art Resource: p. 47; Joseph Martin/Art Resource: p. 88; The Metropolitan Museum of Art, Gift of Nathan Cummings, 1967, #67.167.13: p. 24; National Library of Medicine: pp. 19, 32; Judy Rosemann/Art Resource: p. 82; Andrew Saks/Art Resource: p. 37; Manu Sassoonian/Art Resource: p. 96; Scala/Art Resource: p. 60; Roger B. Smith/Art Resource: p. 62; The Smithsonian Institution/National Anthropological Archive: p. 99; UPI/Bettmann Newsphotos: p. 45; Peter Yates/Art Resource: p. 10

Index

Alan B. Theodore is a freelance writer on medical and health-care subjects. He was formerly vice president-copy supervisor at William Douglas McAdams, Inc., an advertising agency whose clients are leading manufacturers of prescription pharmaceuticals. Currently, Mr. Theodore teaches a course in medical writing at New York University.

Solomon H. Snyder, M.D., is Distinguished Service Professor of Neuroscience, Pharmacology and Psychiatry at The Johns Hopkins University School of Medicine. He has served as president of the Society for Neuroscience and in 1978 received the Albert Lasker Award in Medical Research. He has authored *Uses of Marijuana, Madness and the Brain, The Troubled Mind, Biological Aspects of Mental Disorder,* and edited *Perspective in Neuropharmacology: A Tribute to Julius Axelrod.* Professor Snyder was a research associate with Dr. Axelrod at the National Institutes of Health.

Barry L. Jacobs, Ph.D., is currently a professor in the program of neuroscience at Princeton University. Professor Jacobs is author of *Serotonin Neurotransmission and Behavior* and *Hallucinogens: Neurochemical, Behavioral and Clinical Perspectives.* He has written many journal articles in the field of neuroscience and contributed numerous chapters to books on behavior and brain science. He has been a member of several panels of the National Institute of Mental Health.

Joann Ellison Rodgers, M.S. (Columbia), became Deputy Director of Public Affairs and Director of Media Relations for the Johns Hopkins Medical Institutions in Baltimore, Maryland, in 1984 after 18 years as an award-winning science journalist and widely read columnist for the Hearst newspapers.